THE TRUTH ABOUT

SELF-DOUBT

Secrets to Master Self-Confidence with Easy
Effective Strategies to Unlock Your True Self-
Image in Just Less Than a Year!

Tam Greene

Table of Contents

Download Your Free Gift

Thank you so much for purchasing this book! As a way of saying thanks, I'm offering 2 books "The Power of Thoughts" and "Build Your Thought in 21 Days" for FREE!!!

To get instant access just go to:

https://sozolifebooks.com/

Inside the book, you will discover:

- The master keys to unlocking secrets to peace and mental stability
- A simple powerful step-by-step guide that will produce results in 21 days!
- How this easy change will save you years from mental instability
- And so much more!

If you want to finally achieve a healthy mindset and a brighter future, make sure to grab the free book.

How To Use This Book

I encourage you to read this book at least once. From there, I strongly suggest you revisit this book and focus on specific chapters that you want to explore and go more in-depth.

This book provides a lot of tips and tricks for you to implement and exercise. I don't expect you to go through them all right away, as this is a learning process that you can build upon with time. My hope is for you to pick some that you like and apply them in your life. Keep in mind that the results you'll get out of this book heavily depend on how much time and effort you're willing to put in.

If you see that this book can be of benefit to your friends and family, share it with them! Every person has the potential to be free and be the best version of themselves, and I truly believe that obtaining a deeper understanding of this topic will benefit us all.

INTRODUCTION

"The worst enemy of our humanity is our self-doubt."

— Lolly Daskal

Did you know that self-doubt can be contagious? When we spend time with people who doubt themselves, we can unconsciously adopt their way of thinking and begin to doubt ourselves too. This is because we are social creatures, and our brains are wired to pick up on and mimic the behaviors and attitudes of those around us.

For example, imagine that you are working on a project with a colleague who is constantly second-guessing themselves and expressing self-doubt. Over time, you may begin to internalize their doubts and start to question your own abilities as well. This can lead to a cycle of negative thinking and a lack of confidence that can hold you back in your personal and professional life.

A study published in the Journal of Experimental Social Psychology found that people who were exposed to negative feedback from others were more likely to doubt their own abilities. In this study, participants were asked to complete a task and then received feedback from either a supportive or critical observer. Participants who received critical feedback were more likely to express self-doubt about their abilities and report feeling less confident in their performance than those who received supportive feedback.

Self-doubt can have many different causes, but one common course of self-doubt is negative past experiences. If we have experienced failure, rejection, or criticism in the past, it can create a sense of self-doubt that lingers even after the immediate experience is over.

Several studies support this claim. One of these studies is one published in the Journal of Personality and Social Psychology. The study found that people who experienced negative social feedback (such as rejection, criticism, or failure) were more likely to express self-doubt and have lower self-esteem. The study followed participants over a two-year period and found that those who experienced more negative feedback had greater increases in self-doubt and lower self-esteem over time.

The truth is that we all experience self-doubt in our daily lives. Some of this can be linked to mild self-doubt, where you simply question the possibility of a particular course of action. On the other hand, self-doubt is detrimental when it becomes severe or chronic. This could lead to a constant negative self-image, stress, and anxiety.

Also, self-doubt can make you look down on yourself while totally engrossed in constant comparison and competing with others. This can be so immersive, to the extent that it leaves you with constant negative self-talk about your life and will make you feel as if you've made little to no progress.

Self-doubt also leaves you with the feeling of being less than and lacking, irrespective of your accomplishments. In fact, it doesn't give you room to appreciate what you've accomplished.

Its detrimental character can also overwhelm you with thoughts of inadequacy—a feeling of not doing enough for yourself.

The moment you begin to internalize these negative thoughts and talks, you begin to feel that you may never escape it and that you might have to come to terms with it.

Fortunately, this book is here to help! With this book, you're surely on the right track to finding the long-deserving peace you crave. This book effectively breaks the cycle of self-doubt and creates a healthy self-image.

If you've always wanted to see development, progress, and growth in your life, cheer up because this is exactly what you're getting from this book. You will learn strategies and plans to aid you in the thought and feelings of growth in both your professional and personal life.

Do you want to finally enjoy your life and not get pulled back into the unending cycle of self-doubt? Read on!

CHAPTER 1

UNDERSTANDING

SELF-DOUBT

"When you mark where your self-doubt is, then you can begin to conquer it."

— Stephen Richards

WHAT IS SELF-DOUBT?

Self-doubt refers to a lack of confidence in oneself or one's abilities. It is a feeling of uncertainty or hesitation about one's own decisions, actions, or beliefs. Self-doubt can manifest in

1

different ways, such as second-guessing oneself, feeling inadequate or incompetent, or constantly seeking reassurance or validation from others.

When self-doubt becomes excessive or chronic, it can interfere with one's personal and professional development. It can lead to self-sabotage, indecisiveness, and a reluctance to take risks or pursue opportunities.

According to a study published in the journal "Social Cognitive and Affective Neuroscience" in 2016, self-doubt can lead to decreased activation in the brain's reward system, which can result in a reluctance to take risks and pursue opportunities.

The study aimed to investigate the neural mechanisms underlying the impact of self-doubt on decision-making. The study involved 35 participants who completed a gambling task while their brain activity was monitored using functional magnetic resonance imaging (fMRI).

During the gambling task, participants had to choose between two options with different probabilities of winning or losing money. The researchers manipulated the participants' levels of self-doubt by providing them with either positive or negative feedback on their performance.

The results of the study showed that participants who received negative feedback and reported higher levels of self-doubt had reduced activation in the brain's reward system, specifically in the ventral striatum, which is a region associated with motivation and reward processing. This reduced activation in the reward system was also associated with a reluctance to take risks and a lower likelihood of selecting the option with the highest potential reward.

These findings suggest that self-doubt can interfere with an individual's decision-making abilities by reducing their motivation and willingness to take risks, which can ultimately limit their opportunities for success.

Another study supports the fact that self-doubt can lead to a self-protective mindset that hinders personal growth and development. This is according to the study published in the "Journal of Personality and Social Psychology" in 2015.

The study aimed to investigate how self-doubt can influence an individual's mindset and approach to personal growth and development. The study involved three experiments with a total of 649 participants.

In the first experiment, participants completed a questionnaire that assessed their level of self-doubt and their mindset toward personal growth and development. The results showed that individuals with high levels of self-doubt were more likely to have a "fixed mindset," which is the belief that one's abilities and traits are predetermined and cannot be changed through effort or learning.

In the second experiment, participants were randomly assigned to receive either a fixed mindset or a growth mindset intervention. The results showed that the growth mindset intervention was effective in reducing self-doubt and increasing motivation toward personal growth and development.

In the third experiment, participants completed a task that required them to think creatively and generate new ideas. The results showed that individuals with high levels of self-doubt were less likely to think creatively and generate new concepts compared to individuals with low levels of self-doubt.

Overall, the study suggests that self-doubt can lead to a fixed mindset and a reluctance to engage in personal growth and development, which can ultimately limit an individual's potential for success.

TRIGGERS OF SELF-DOUBT

Self-doubt can be triggered by various factors, and the effects on individuals can vary, depending on the severity and duration of the self-doubt.

Here are some common triggers of self-doubt:

Past Failures or Criticisms

Past failures or criticisms refer to negative feedback, criticism, or failure in the past that can trigger self-doubt in individuals. These experiences can make individuals feel inadequate or incompetent, leading to a lack of confidence and motivation and a reluctance to take risks or pursue opportunities.

For example, if someone has failed to meet a deadline at work, they may start to doubt their abilities and worry that they are not competent enough to succeed in their job.

Similarly, if someone receives negative feedback on a creative project or personal goal, they may start to doubt their skills and believe they are not good enough to achieve their aspirations.

Campbell & Sedikides (1999) backed up this claim in their study published in the "Journal of Personality and Social Psychology." The study examined the relationship between past criticisms and negative self-talk and beliefs.

It involved two experiments. In the first experiment, participants were asked to recall a specific criticism they had received in the past, either from a close friend or a stranger. They were then asked to complete a series of measures assessing their negative self-talk, negative self-beliefs, and self-esteem. The results showed that individuals who had recalled past criticisms were more likely to engage in negative self-talk and to have negative self-beliefs than those who had not recalled past criticisms. Additionally, the effect of past criticism was stronger for individuals who were more self-critical.

In the second experiment, the researchers manipulated the level of self-esteem of participants by providing either positive or negative feedback on their performance in a task. Participants were then asked to recall a specific criticism or praise they had received in the past and to complete the same measures as in the first experiment. The results showed that individuals who received negative feedback and recalled past criticisms had significantly lower self-esteem and more negative self-beliefs than those who received negative feedback but recalled past praise or those who received positive feedback.

Overall, the study suggests that past criticisms can have a lasting impact on individuals' self-talk and beliefs, leading to a negative self-image and lower self-esteem.

From this, we've seen that past failures or criticisms can have a significant impact on an individual's self-esteem and confidence, especially if they are not addressed or resolved. Over time, these negative experiences can create a pattern of self-doubt and self-sabotage, where individuals may feel like they are not capable of succeeding and therefore do not try.

Unrealistic Expectations

Unrealistic expectations refer to setting goals or standards that are too high or unattainable, which can trigger self-doubt in individuals. When individuals set unrealistic expectations, they may feel like they are not measuring up or achieving their goals, which can lead to feelings of inadequacy, imposter syndrome, and a negative self-image.

Several studies have shown that unrealistic expectations can lead to self-doubt and decreased self-esteem. For example, a study published in the journal "Motivation and Emotion" found that individuals who set high expectations for themselves and had low self-esteem were more likely to experience self-doubt and negative emotions when they failed to meet their goals (Kornadt & Kandler, 2017).

Another study published in the "Journal of Personality and Social Psychology" found that unrealistic expectations can also lead to procrastination, as individuals may feel overwhelmed and unsure of how to achieve their goals (Koestner & Losier, 2002).

This study, conducted by Koestner and Losier in 2002, examined the relationship between unrealistic expectations and procrastination. The researchers found that individuals who set unrealistic goals for themselves were more likely to procrastinate, as they felt overwhelmed and unsure of how to achieve their goals.

The study involved 165 undergraduate students who completed a questionnaire on their goal-setting strategies and tendency to procrastinate. The results showed that individuals who set high, unrealistic goals for themselves were more likely to procrastinate compared to those who set more realistic goals.

The researchers suggested that setting unrealistic expectations can lead to a sense of failure and self-doubt, which in turn can lead to procrastination. This can create a cycle where individuals continue to set unrealistic goals but are unable to achieve them, leading to further self-doubt and procrastination.

Perfectionism

Perfectionism is a personality trait characterized by setting high and unrealistic standards for oneself and striving for flawless performance. Perfectionists often feel a constant need to achieve excellence, and they are highly critical of themselves when they fall short of their expectations. While perfectionism can lead to positive outcomes, such as increased motivation and productivity, it can also be associated with negative outcomes, such as self-doubt, anxiety, and depression.

Research has shown that perfectionism is strongly linked to self-doubt. One study conducted by Hewitt and Flett (1991) found that perfectionism was associated with increased self-criticism, fear of failure, and negative feedback.

The study examined the relationship between perfectionism and psychological distress in university students. The researchers were particularly interested in examining how two different types of perfectionism, self-oriented perfectionism and socially prescribed perfectionism, were related to negative outcomes, such as self-criticism, fear of failure, and negative feedback.

9

To conduct the study, the researchers recruited 238 undergraduate students from a Canadian university. The participants completed a series of questionnaires that assessed their levels of perfectionism, psychological distress, and other related constructs.

The first questionnaire measured the participants' levels of perfectionism using the Multidimensional Perfectionism Scale (MPS). This scale assesses three dimensions of perfectionism: self-oriented perfectionism (setting high standards for oneself), other-oriented perfectionism (setting high standards for others), and socially prescribed perfectionism (perceiving high standards from others). For this study, the researchers focused on the self-oriented and socially prescribed dimensions of perfectionism.

The second questionnaire measured the participants' levels of psychological distress using the Symptom Checklist-90-R (SCL-90-R). This scale assesses a broad range of psychological symptoms, including anxiety, depression, and interpersonal sensitivity.

The results of the study showed that both self-oriented and socially prescribed perfectionism were significantly related to increased psychological distress. Specifically, self-oriented perfectionism was associated with increased self-criticism and fear of failure, while socially prescribed perfectionism was associated with increased negative feedback.

The study provides evidence for the link between perfectionism and negative outcomes such as self-doubt and psychological distress. It suggests that both types of perfectionism can lead to negative consequences.

Similarly, another study conducted by Stoeber and Otto (2006) found that perfectionism was associated with higher levels of self-doubt, and this was especially true for individuals who had high personal standards but were unable to meet them.

The researchers of this study were interested in examining how different aspects of perfectionism, such as personal standards and self-critical tendencies, were related to self-doubt in university students.

To conduct the study, the researchers recruited 187 undergraduate students from a British university. The participants completed a series of questionnaires that assessed their levels of perfectionism, self-doubt, and related constructs.

The first questionnaire measured the participants' levels of perfectionism using the Multidimensional Perfectionism Scale

(MPS), which assesses three dimensions of perfectionism: self-oriented perfectionism, other-oriented perfectionism, and socially prescribed perfectionism. The researchers focused on the self-oriented dimension of perfectionism for this study, which measures the extent to which individuals set high personal standards for themselves.

The second questionnaire measured the participants' levels of self-doubt using the Self-Doubt Scale (SDS). This scale assesses the frequency and intensity of self-doubt experiences in different domains, such as academic performance and social interactions.

The study's results revealed that self-oriented perfectionism was significantly related to higher levels of self-doubt. Specifically, individuals with high personal standards who could not meet them experienced more self-doubt than those who had lower personal standards. The researchers also found that self-critical tendencies mediated the relationship between self-oriented perfectionism and self-doubt.

Overall, the study provides evidence for the link between perfectionism and self-doubt and highlights the importance of examining different aspects of perfectionism in understanding this relationship. It suggests that individuals who have high personal standards but struggle to meet them are particularly vulnerable to self-doubt and that self-critical tendencies play a role in this relationship.

Comparison to Others

Comparison to others is a common cause of self-doubt. When we compare ourselves to others, we may perceive ourselves as falling short or not measuring up to the standards of others, which can lead to feelings of inadequacy and self-doubt. There is scientific evidence to support the link between comparison to others and self-doubt.

One study conducted by Festinger (1954) found that social comparison plays a crucial role in shaping our self-concept and self-evaluation. Festinger proposed that individuals evaluate their own abilities and opinions by comparing them to those of others. In particular, individuals tend to compare themselves to others who are similar to them in terms of relevant attributes, such as intelligence, physical attractiveness, and academic performance.

Another study by Buunk et al. (1993) examined the relationship between upward social comparison (comparing oneself to those who are perceived as better off) and self-esteem. The researchers found that upward social comparison was associated with lower self-esteem, particularly among individuals who had low self-esteem to begin with. The study suggests that comparing oneself to others who are perceived as better off can lead to negative self-evaluation and self-doubt.

Similarly, a study by Zell and Alicke (2013) found that upward social comparison was associated with feelings of inferiority and self-doubt, particularly among individuals who had a strong desire to improve themselves. The researchers found that individuals who engaged in upward social comparison were more likely to doubt their abilities and feel inadequate compared to others.

Overall, these studies provide evidence for the link between comparison to others and self-doubt. They suggest that upward social comparison, in particular, can lead to negative self-evaluation and feelings of inadequacy, particularly among individuals who have low self-esteem or a strong desire to improve themselves.

Trauma or Past Experiences

Trauma or past experiences can also trigger self-doubt. Experiencing a traumatic event or a negative experience can undermine one's confidence, sense of self-worth, and ability to trust oneself. This can lead to self-doubt and a lack of confidence in one's abilities and decision-making skills.

One relatable story of someone who developed self-doubt as a result of past trauma is the case of Emily, who experienced emotional abuse from a family member during her childhood. The abuse led to her feeling worthless and undeserving of love and care. As a result, she developed self-doubt and struggled with making decisions, trusting others, and asserting herself.

Research has shown that traumatic events can have a significant impact on one's self-esteem and confidence. A study by Frewen et al. (2011) found that individuals who had experienced trauma were more likely to have lower self-esteem and higher levels of self-criticism and self-doubt than those who had not experienced trauma. The study also found that the severity of the trauma was related to the extent of self-criticism and self-doubt.

Another study by Brenner et al. (2019) examined the relationship between adverse childhood experiences (ACEs) and self-doubt in adults. ACEs are defined as potentially traumatic events that occur in childhood, such as physical, sexual, or emotional abuse, neglect, or household dysfunction.

The study found that individuals who had experienced ACEs were more likely to have higher levels of self-doubt and lower levels of self-esteem than those who had not experienced ACEs.

This particular study was carried out on 385 participants who completed a survey measuring ACEs, self-doubt, and self-esteem. The researchers found that individuals who had experienced ACEs were more likely to have higher levels of self-doubt and lower levels of self-esteem than those who had not experienced ACEs. The study also found that the severity of the ACEs was related to the extent of self-doubt and self-esteem.

Specifically, the study found that emotional abuse and neglect were the ACEs most strongly associated with self-doubt and lower self-esteem. Physical and sexual abuse were also associated with higher levels of self-doubt and lower self-esteem but to a lesser extent than emotional abuse and neglect.

The researchers concluded that experiencing ACEs can have a lasting impact on one's confidence and self-esteem, leading to self-doubt and a lack of trust in oneself.

REMEMBER: Self-doubt is a common human feeling and can help people exercise caution and deep consideration before acting. However, severe or persistent self-doubt might obstruct one's progress in life. It may cause you to undermine your own efforts, be unable to make decisions, and prevent you from grabbing opportunities that present themselves.

SELF-IMAGE: WHAT ROLE DOES IT PLAY IN SELF-DOUBT?

The way we perceive ourselves, also known as self-image, is not innate or fixed. Rather, it is shaped by a combination of our experiences, relationships, and environment. Self-image can be taught, created, and nurtured throughout our lives, and it is heavily influenced by what we were taught as we were growing up.

Our self-image, or how we see ourselves, is influenced by the messages and feedback we receive from those around us. When we receive positive feedback and validation from others, we are more likely to have a positive self-image and feel confident in our abilities. However, when we receive negative feedback or criticism, particularly from important individuals such as parents, siblings, or peers, this can lead to self-doubt and a negative self-image.

For example, if a child consistently receives criticism from their parents or siblings for their academic performance or physical

17

appearance, they may begin to internalize these messages and believe that they are not smart or attractive enough. Similarly, if a teenager is consistently teased or bullied by their peers, they may begin to believe that they are unlikable or unpopular.

These negative messages can become deeply ingrained in our self-perception and can lead to self-doubt and low self-esteem. This can manifest in a variety of ways, such as a fear of failure, a lack of confidence in social situations, or difficulty asserting oneself in relationships or at work.

In addition to external messages, our self-image is also shaped by our internal beliefs and perceptions. Our thoughts, emotions, and attitudes all contribute to how we see ourselves. For example, if a person tends to focus on their flaws and shortcomings, they may develop a negative self-image, even if they have received positive messages from others.

It is important to note that self-image is not set in stone. With conscious effort and practice, we can change how we see ourselves and improve our self-image.

The good news is that you've found this book. Gradually, your self-doubt will soon be a thing of the past.

Key Takeaways

In this chapter, we've been able to learn the following:

- What is self-doubt?
- Triggers of self-doubt
- The role of self-image in self-doubt

In the next chapter, we're going to look at the signs and symptoms of self-doubt and how to know if you doubt yourself. It is only when you can identify the symptoms of self-doubt that you can be certain that you're experiencing it. So, let's find out!

CHAPTER 2

THE SIGNS AND SYMPTOMS OF SELF-DOUBT

"Our doubts are traitors and make us lose the good we oft might win by fearing to attempt."
— William Shakespeare

Self-doubt is a pervasive feeling that can affect anyone, regardless of age, gender, or background. It can manifest in various ways, from feeling unsure about your abilities to questioning your decisions and choices. It can be caused by

21

various factors, such as past experiences, trauma, and comparison to others. Whatever the cause, self-doubt can be a significant obstacle to living the life you want.

Many people may not even realize they are experiencing self-doubt, as it can be mistaken for other emotions or behaviors. However, it's essential to recognize the signs of self-doubt to overcome them and move forward with confidence. In this chapter, we will delve deeper into the common signs of self-doubt.

Whether you're struggling with self-doubt in your personal or professional life, this guide will help you recognize the symptoms so that you can take steps towards a more confident and fulfilling life.

COMMON SIGNS AND SYMPTOMS OF SELF-DOUBT

Indecisiveness

Indecisiveness is a common symptom of self-doubt and can manifest in various ways. When you're unsure of yourself, it's easy to get stuck in a cycle of indecision, which can cause you to miss out on opportunities or delay important decisions. You may struggle to make decisions or second-guess the ones you've made.

For example, someone experiencing self-doubt may have difficulty deciding on a career path. They may be uncertain about their abilities or qualifications and are unsure about their future. As a result, they may delay making decisions, leading to missed opportunities or a lack of direction in their career.

Similarly, someone experiencing self-doubt may have difficulty making decisions in their personal life, such as where to live or whom to date. They may doubt their ability to make the right choice and fear making the wrong one. This indecisiveness can lead to missed opportunities, missed experiences, and a general feeling of being stuck.

There has been numerous research that backs up this claim. One of these is the Journal of Personality and Social Psychology. The researchers conducted a series of experiments with participants and analyzed their decision-making behaviors and levels of self-doubt.

The results of the study indicated that individuals who experienced higher levels of self-doubt tended to be more indecisive when making decisions. The researchers suggested that this was because self-doubt can create uncertainty and anxiety, making it difficult for people to make a choice. The fear of making the wrong decision can also lead to prolonged indecision and overthinking.

One of the experiments involved participants making choices between different options. The researchers found that those with higher levels of self-doubt took longer to make decisions and were less confident in their choices than those with lower levels of self-doubt.

The study also highlighted that the relationship between self-doubt and indecisiveness was moderated by the complexity of the decision-making task. In more straightforward decisions, self-doubt did not have a significant impact on decision-making. However, in more complex decisions, individuals with higher levels of self-doubt were more likely to be indecisive.

Avoidance

Avoidance is another common sign and symptom of self-doubt. When you doubt yourself, you may avoid situations or tasks that you perceive as challenging or risky. You may fear failure, rejection, or embarrassment and believe that it's better not to try at all than to risk experiencing these negative outcomes.

Avoidance can manifest in various ways. For example, you may avoid making a significant financial investment or expressing your opinions, trying new things or taking on new responsibilities, or avoiding social situations that require you to interact with new people.

Avoidance can be detrimental to your personal and professional growth, leading to missed opportunities for learning and development. It can also cause guilt, shame, and low self-esteem, further perpetuating self-doubt.

Procrastination

Procrastination is another common symptom of self-doubt. When you doubt yourself, you may procrastinate on tasks or projects that require you to take action. You may fear that you won't be able to complete the task successfully or that you'll make mistakes. As a result, you may delay starting or completing the task, which can lead to increased stress and anxiety.

Procrastination can manifest in various ways. For example, imagine a student who struggles with math and has received poor grades in the past. They have an upcoming math exam, but instead of studying, they find themselves procrastinating and avoiding the material. They may feel overwhelmed and doubt

25

their ability to understand the concepts, leading them to put off studying until the last minute.

As the exam approaches, their procrastination may intensify, leading to increased feelings of anxiety and self-doubt. They may feel guilty and ashamed for not studying earlier, which can further reinforce negative beliefs about their ability to succeed in math.

Procrastination can also create a self-fulfilling cycle of self-doubt and failure. When someone procrastinates, they may end up rushing to complete a task or turning in subpar work, which can lead to poor outcomes and reinforce feelings of inadequacy. This can create a pattern of further procrastination and underperformance, which can erode confidence and self-esteem over time.

Negative body image

Self-doubt can manifest in negative body image in a variety of ways. Negative body image refers to the perception that one's body is inadequate or flawed in some way, which can lead to feelings of shame, embarrassment, and low self-esteem.

When someone is experiencing self-doubt, they may begin to question their worth and value as a person. This can lead to a preoccupation with their physical appearance and a tendency to focus on perceived flaws or imperfections. They may become overly critical of their body, compare themselves unfavorably to others, or have unrealistic standards of beauty and perfection.

Negative body image can also manifest as a result of social comparison. Social media and advertising often present images of "perfect" bodies, which can lead to feelings of inadequacy and self-doubt. When someone is already struggling with self-doubt, these images can exacerbate negative body image, leading to anxiety and depression.

Negative body image can have a significant impact on mental health and well-being. It can lead to disordered eating behaviors, such as binge eating or restrictive eating, and can contribute to the development of eating disorders such as anorexia or bulimia. This is further buttressed by a 2020 review published in the journal "Nutrients." The review analyzed 101 studies that investigated this relationship, including both cross-sectional and longitudinal studies.

The review found that negative body image was a significant risk factor for disordered eating behaviors and eating disorders in both men and women. Specifically, the review found that negative body image was associated with a higher risk of binge eating, purging, restrictive eating, and other disordered eating behaviors.

Negative body image can also lead to avoidance of social situations, exercise, and other activities that may exacerbate feelings of self-doubt. This is because when someone has a negative body image, they may feel self-conscious and insecure about their appearance, which can lead to a fear of being judged or criticized by others, especially in social situations that require them to be seen or evaluated by others. As a result, they may avoid social situations altogether to avoid the potential negative feelings that can arise from these interactions.

In addition, someone with a negative body image may avoid exercise or physical activity because they feel uncomfortable or embarrassed about their body. This can lead to a sedentary lifestyle, which can exacerbate negative feelings about their body and lead to a cycle of inactivity and decreased self-esteem.

Fear of failure

Fear of failure is a common phenomenon experienced by many individuals when faced with the possibility of not achieving a desired outcome. It is often associated with feelings of anxiety, nervousness, and uncertainty. One of the underlying causes of this fear is self-doubt, which is defined as a lack of confidence in oneself and one's abilities.

For example, imagine a student who is afraid to take a test because they are worried about failing. This fear of failure may stem from self-doubt about their ability to perform well on the test. The student may doubt their own knowledge and skills, which can lead to anxiety and avoidance of that test.

In this scenario, the fear of failure is a sign of self-doubt because the student is not confident in their ability to do well. If the student had more confidence in themselves, they may not feel as fearful about the possibility of failure and may be more likely to approach the test with a positive attitude.

Research has consistently shown that fear of failure is closely linked to self-doubt. A study titled "Fear of Failure and Achievement Goals in University Students," conducted by Dr. Martin Covington and his colleagues and published in the journal, "Journal of Educational Psychology" in 1997, found that students who experience self-doubt are more likely to have a fear of failure than those who have confidence in their abilities. The study also showed that fear of failure could lead to decreased motivation and performance, particularly among students who are highly self-doubting.

Another study, "Implicit Theories and Their Role in Judgments and Reactions: A World from Two Perspectives," conducted by Dr. Carol Dweck and her colleagues and published in the journal, "Psychological Inquiry," in 1993, found that individuals who have a fixed mindset (the belief that one's abilities are fixed and cannot be changed) are more likely to experience fear of failure than those who have a growth mindset (the belief that one's abilities can be developed through effort and hard work). The study also showed that individuals with a growth mindset were more likely to view failure as a learning opportunity rather than as a reflection of their abilities.

Negative self-talk

Negative self-talk is a common symptom of self-doubt. It refers to the habit of engaging in critical or pessimistic self-talk, which can be a symptom of self-doubt. It involves internalizing negative thoughts and beliefs about oneself, one's abilities, and one's potential. According to research, negative self-talk can significantly impact an individual's mental health and self-esteem, leading to self-doubt, anxiety, depression, and low self-worth (Marshall et al., 2015).

For example, let's consider a scenario where a person is struggling with self-doubt about their ability to perform well in a new job. This person might engage in negative self-talk, such as, "I'm not smart enough for this job," "I'll never be able to keep up with my coworkers," or "I'm going to mess up and get fired." These thoughts are not only unhelpful but can also be damaging to the person's self-confidence and ability to perform in their job.

Over time, negative self-talk can become a self-fulfilling prophecy, as the person's belief in their inadequacy can lead to behaviors that reinforce their negative beliefs. In this example, the person's self-doubt and negative self-talk may cause them to avoid taking on new tasks or seek out help from coworkers, limiting their growth and development in the job.

NOTE: Self-doubt can manifest in various signs and symptoms, such as indecisiveness, negative self-talk, and fear of failure. Recognizing these signs is the first step toward building self-confidence.

TRAITS AND RESPONSES OF PEOPLE IN SELF-DOUBT

People who are struggling with self-doubt often share common traits. Below are some traits and how they might manifest in people experiencing self-doubt. Similar to the signs and symptoms of self-doubt, if you fall within any of these, know you're experiencing self-doubt.

TRAIT	HOW IT MIGHT MANIFEST
Negative self-talk	Talking down to themselves, doubting their abilities, or being overly critical of themselves. E.g., "I can never do anything right." "I don't think I am the right person for this job." "I am going to make a mistake performing this task."
Perfectionism	Being overly focused on details, struggling to finish tasks or projects, or becoming frustrated when things don't go as planned.
Avoidance	Procrastinating, delaying decision-making, or avoiding social situations or activities that might put them in the spotlight.

Overthinking	Getting stuck in a loop of analyzing past mistakes, worrying excessively about the future, or ruminating on negative thoughts.
Self-sabotage	Intentionally undermining their own success or progress, procrastinating on important tasks, or avoiding opportunities for growth.
Imposter syndrome	Feeling like a fraud, doubting their own accomplishments, or feeling like they don't deserve recognition or success.
Seeking reassurance	Constantly looking for validation from others, seeking approval or praise for their actions or decisions, or needing external feedback to feel secure.
Indecisiveness	Struggling to make decisions, feeling overwhelmed by choices, or constantly second-guessing themselves.

Lack of confidence	Struggling to speak up in a group, not believing in their own abilities, or feeling uncomfortable in new or unfamiliar situations.
Fear of failure	Avoiding challenges or opportunities for growth, feeling stuck in a comfort zone, or not taking risks.

REMEMBER: Self-doubt is a common experience that many people face at some point in their lives. It has common traits, such as perfectionism, avoidance, overthinking, self-sabotage, fear of failure, lack of confidence, indecisiveness, seeking reassurance, and imposter syndrome. These traits can cause individuals to feel stuck, overwhelmed, and unsure of themselves, leading to a lack of progress and growth in various areas of life. It's important to recognize these traits to put yourself on the right track and regain your self-confidence and peace of mind.

Key Takeaways

We've successfully learned the following:

- Common signs and symptoms of self-doubt

- Traits and responses of people in self-doubt

Now that you know how to recognize self-doubt through its signs and symptoms, you can move on to the next chapter, where you will learn about comparing and competing mentalities. This will help you understand how self-doubt unnecessarily bears the mentality of comparison and competition. Eager to learn? Read on!

CHAPTER 3

OVER-COMPARING AND COMPETING

"Other people's lives seem better than yours because you're comparing their director's cuts with your behind the scenes."

— Evan Rauch

WHAT DOES IT MEAN TO OVER COMPARE AND COMPETE?

In today's world, it is all too easy to get caught up in the cycle of over-comparing and competing. Social media, advertising, and even our peers and colleagues can all contribute to a constant feeling of not measuring up or needing to do more.

37

However, constantly comparing ourselves to others and competing with them can be detrimental to our mental health and well-being.

When we compare ourselves to others, we often focus on what we lack instead of our own strengths and accomplishments. This can lead to feelings of inadequacy and low self-esteem. Moreover, we tend to compare ourselves to others based on external factors such as looks, possessions, or achievements rather than our own internal values and goals.

On the other hand, when we engage in constant competition, we may become overly consumed with winning and lose sight of the bigger picture. We may also become too preoccupied with others' success and feel threatened by it, instead of being motivated and inspired by it.

Additionally, over-comparing and competing can lead to burnout, stress, and anxiety. When we constantly strive to do more, be better, and achieve more, we may neglect our own self-care and well-being. We may also feel like we are never enough or that we are always falling behind, which can lead to stress, overwhelming emotions, and self-doubt.

THE RESULTS OF SELF-DOUBT

Over-comparing and competing

Over-comparing and competing is a result of self-doubt. When we engage in these behaviors to an excessive degree, it can be a sign that our self-esteem is fragile and we are seeking external validation to feel good about ourselves. This can lead to a cycle of constant comparison and competition, which can be detrimental to our mental health and well-being.

Research has shown that over-comparing and competing can be linked to a range of negative outcomes, including anxiety, depression, and low self-esteem. In a review of studies on social comparison and well-being, researchers found that "people who engage in more upward social comparison, that is, comparing oneself to someone perceived to be better off, tend to have lower levels of self-esteem and subjective well-being" (Festinger, 1954; Taylor & Lobel, 1989; Wood et al., 1989).

Similarly, a study on competitive behavior and psychological well-being found that "individuals who perceive themselves as more competitive also tend to report higher levels of anxiety, depression, and other psychological disorders" (Kohn & Schooler, 1983). The study also found that excessive competitiveness can lead to social isolation and interpersonal conflicts, which can further exacerbate feelings of self-doubt and insecurity.

Low self-esteem and self-worth

Low self-esteem and low self-worth are common consequences of over-comparing and competing because constantly comparing ourselves to others and striving to be better can make us feel like we are not good enough. When we focus on the achievements and successes of others, we may start to feel like we are falling short or not measuring up.

Imagine a professional athlete who is constantly comparing their performance to that of their teammates or competitors. They may feel like they are not as fast or strong as others, which can lead to feelings of inadequacy and low self-esteem. Additionally, they may become overly focused on winning and being the best, which can cause them to lose the joy of the sport and their own personal growth.

Another good example is that of a student who is always comparing their grades to their classmates and feels like they are not as smart or talented as others. The student may start to believe that they are not capable of achieving the same level of success as their peers, which can lead to negative self-talk and a lack of confidence.

Over time, this negative mindset can become deeply ingrained, leading to a sense of learned helplessness and a lack of motivation to try new things or take risks. The student may start to believe that they are not worthy of success or happiness, which can have a long-lasting impact on their mental health and well-being.

In this way, low self-esteem and self-worth are a consequence of over-comparing and competing because they are the result of constantly measuring ourselves against others and feeling like we are not good enough.

Stress and anxiety

Stress and anxiety can be caused by a number of factors, and one of them is the tendency to over compare and compete with others. This can happen in various areas of life, such as work, relationships, or social situations.

When we constantly compare ourselves to others, we may feel pressure to perform better or achieve more in order to measure up to them. This can create a sense of inadequacy, leading to feelings of stress and anxiety. Similarly, when we focus too much on competing with others, we may experience constant pressure to outdo them, which can be both mentally and physically exhausting.

Moreover, when we engage in constant comparisons and competition, we may lose sight of our own values and goals. Instead of focusing on what we want to achieve for our own fulfillment, we become preoccupied with the achievements of others, which can create a sense of emptiness and dissatisfaction.

Overall, while a healthy level of competition and comparison can be motivating, excessive comparison and competition can be detrimental to our mental health and well-being, leading to increased stress and anxiety.

Limited perspective and growth

Over-comparing and competing can lead to limited perspective and growth in several ways:

Firstly, constantly comparing ourselves to others can cause us to focus primarily on external factors, such as others' achievements, possessions, or social status. By doing this, we may lose sight of our own unique strengths and weaknesses, which can limit our ability to develop and grow as individuals. For example, if we are constantly comparing ourselves to a more successful colleague at work, we may overlook our own unique talents and abilities that could help us excel in our own way.

Secondly, competing with others can cause us to become overly focused on short-term wins, rather than long-term goals and aspirations. We may be so preoccupied with outdoing others that we fail to see the bigger picture or consider alternative approaches that could be more effective. This can limit our ability to explore new opportunities and experiences, as we may be too focused on beating the competition to take risks and try new things.

Thirdly, comparing ourselves to others can lead to feelings of inadequacy, low self-esteem, and self-doubt, which can further limit our growth and potential. When we constantly measure ourselves against others, we may develop unrealistic expectations of ourselves and become overly critical of our own accomplishments. This can erode our self-confidence and prevent us from pursuing our goals with enthusiasm and determination.

Overall, over-comparing and competing can be detrimental to our personal growth and development by limiting our perspective and preventing us from exploring new opportunities and experiences.

Relationship issues

Over-comparing and competing can lead to relationship issues because it creates an environment of constant comparison and evaluation, which can be exhausting and demotivating for both partners.

When a couple constantly compares their relationship to that of their friends, it could become unhealthy and lead to self-doubt as they will begin to have doubts about the future of their relationship or about the possibility of things getting better.

Consider a woman named Maria who has been in a committed relationship with her partner, James, for several years. One day, she meets up with a friend who has just started dating someone new. The friend gushes about how perfect her new partner is, how attentive and romantic he is, and how much they have in common.

As Maria listens to her friend talk, she begins to feel envious and insecure about her own relationship with James. She starts to compare her relationship to her friend's and feels like it doesn't measure up. She starts to wonder if she and James have enough in common, if he's attentive enough, and if she's settling for less than she deserves.

Over time, Maria begins to dwell on these negative thoughts and starts to withdraw from James. She becomes more critical and demanding, expecting him to live up to the idealized version of a partner she has in her head. James senses her growing dissatisfaction and starts to feel frustrated and unappreciated.

Eventually, the strain becomes too much, and Maria and James' relationship begins to break down. Maria realizes too late that her constant comparison to her friend's relationship was unfair and unrealistic, and that she had been projecting her insecurities onto her relationship.

In this example, Maria's constant comparison and competition with her friend's relationship created a sense of insecurity and dissatisfaction in her own relationship. By focusing on what she perceived as the shortcomings of her relationship, she neglected to appreciate the good things about it and ultimately pushed James away.

THE COMPARISON AND COMPETING MENTALITY: HOW DOES IT RELATE TO SELF-DOUBT?

Over-comparing, competing, and self-doubt can be interconnected and can reinforce one another in a negative cycle.

When you constantly compare yourself to others, especially in areas where you perceive them to be more successful, accomplished, or talented, it can create feelings of inadequacy and self-doubt. This is because you are constantly measuring yourself against an external standard rather than focusing on your own progress and growth.

Additionally, when you engage in excessive competition, it can intensify the pressure you put on yourself to perform and succeed. This pressure can lead to increased self-doubt as you worry about not measuring up to your own or others' expectations.

Furthermore, over-comparing and competing can also lead to jealousy or resentment towards others who you perceive as doing better than you. This can further fuel self-doubt and undermine your confidence in your own abilities.

Below are a few examples of how this can play out:

COMPARISON	WHAT IS IT?	MINDSET
Social Media Comparison	Social media platforms, like Instagram and Facebook, can be breeding grounds for comparison and competition. We may see other people's highlight reels and feel like we are falling short in comparison. This can lead to self-doubt and a negative self-image.	John is a college student who spends a lot of time on Twitter. He follows many of his classmates and sees them posting about their internships, job offers, and academic achievements. John begins to compare himself to his classmates and feels like he is falling behind. He starts to doubt his abilities and potential for success, making it difficult for him to stay motivated and focused on his own goals.

| Academic or professional comparisons | In school or at work, we may feel like we are in competition with our peers. We may compare our grades, test scores, or performance evaluations to others and feel like we are not measuring up. This can lead to self-doubt about our abilities and potential. | Jane is a graduate student who is pursuing a Ph.D. in neuroscience. She frequently compares herself to her peers and colleagues, who seem to be publishing more papers and receiving more accolades than she is. She also compares herself to her advisor, who is a renowned scientist in their field. This leads her to feel like she's not good enough and that she's not making enough progress in her research. |

Physical comparisons	Physical comparison is when individuals compare their physical appearances, such as body shape, size, or beauty, to others. This can lead to self-doubt and a negative body image if one feels like they don't measure up to society's beauty standards or other people's appearances. It can also contribute to low self-esteem and a negative self-image.	Emily is a teenager who enjoys spending time with her friends and family. She's noticed that some of her peers seem to get a lot of attention for their physical appearance, with comments like "You're so pretty" or "I wish I looked like you." This sometimes makes Emily feel like she's not as attractive as her friends. She begins to dwell on these thoughts and eventually ends up doubting her beauty.

| Relationship comparisons | Relationship comparison is when individuals compare their romantic relationships or love life to others. This can lead to self-doubt and feelings of inadequacy if one feels like their relationship is not as good as other people's relationships or if they are not currently in a relationship. It can also contribute to low self-esteem and a negative self-image, particularly in the context of social pressure, which may force individuals to be in romantic relationships. | Jessica is a young woman who has never been in a serious relationship. She sees all of her friends dating and getting married and starts to feel like she is behind or missing out. She starts to doubt her own ability to attract a partner and wonders if there is something wrong with her. She feels like she is not lovable and begins to feel insecure about her worth as a person. |

HOW TO CATCH YOURSELF COMPARING AND COMPETING

1. You feel constantly anxious or stressed about how you measure up to others

Feeling constantly anxious or stressed about how you measure up to others means that you are always worried about whether you are as successful, talented, attractive, or accomplished as other people in your life. This can lead to feelings of insecurity and self-doubt, which can have a negative impact on your mental health and overall well-being.

For example, John is always comparing himself to his friend Mark. Mark is a successful lawyer with a large house, a fancy car, and a loving family. John, on the other hand, works a regular 9-5 job and rents a small apartment. Whenever John sees Mark's accomplishments or hears about his latest promotion or expensive vacation, he feels anxious and stressed about whether he is as successful as Mark. He starts to doubt his abilities and believes he is not good enough.

This constant comparison causes John to feel unhappy and unsatisfied with his life, despite the fact that he has many things to be proud of.

2. You experience feelings of jealousy or envy when you see others succeeding

Feeling jealous or envious when you see others succeeding means you are not able to genuinely feel happy for other people's achievements because you are too focused on your shortcomings. This can lead to bitterness and resentment towards others, which can have a negative impact on your relationships and overall happiness.

A good instance of this is the case of a woman, let's say her name is Sarah. Sarah is constantly comparing herself to her coworker, Jane. Jane has just been promoted to a higher position at work and received a significant raise. Instead of feeling genuinely happy about Jane's success, Sarah feels jealous and envious. She starts to think about how she's been working at the company longer than Jane and how she deserves a promotion just as much as Jane does. She can't help but compare her own career progress to Jane's and feels resentful toward her coworker.

This example shows that Sarah is guilty of over-comparing and competing, which ends up leaving her with nothing but negative thoughts and feelings toward Jane. This can eventually make it difficult for Sarah to have a positive working relationship with Jane.

3. You find yourself constantly checking social media or comparing your life to others online.

With the rise of social media platforms, it has become easier than ever to see a curated view of other people's lives, often highlighting their accomplishments, adventures, and happy moments. This can lead to self-doubt (when you begin to doubt your hard work and commitment and feel they aren't enough to give you the kind of life your peers are living). With this comes the feeling of inadequacy, envy, or FOMO (fear of missing out).

For example, Joan, who is active on social media, follows many people who post pictures of their travel experiences, luxury purchases, and exciting social lives. Joan is constantly scrolling through her feeds and comparing her life to what she sees online. She feels she is missing out on fun experiences and wonders why her life doesn't look as exciting or glamorous as those she follows. As a result, she begins to doubt her effort and feels all her years of commitment are a waste. This eventually leads her to feel unhappy or dissatisfied with her life.

NOTE: This constant comparison can be harmful because it often presents a distorted view of reality. People tend to post their best moments online, which can give the impression that their lives are perfect when, in fact, everyone has their own struggles and challenges.

4. You avoid situations where you may be compared to others, such as social events or work meetings

This can happen when we feel insecure or anxious about being judged or evaluated by others, or when we fear that we will not measure up to the standards of others.

Here's an example to illustrate this:

Samantha is a recent college graduate who just started a new job in a competitive industry. She is excited to learn and grow in her new role but feels intimidated by some of her coworkers who have more experience and seem to be more confident. Samantha often avoids team meetings or social events outside of work because she is afraid of being compared to her colleagues and seen as inferior. She worries that she will make mistakes or say something stupid and that her coworkers will judge her harshly.

This avoidance behavior can be problematic because it can prevent us from growing and learning.

5. You engage in negative self-talk or self-criticism, focusing on your flaws or shortcomings instead of your strengths and accomplishments

One of the easiest ways we are found guilty of comparing and competing is through negative self-talk or self-criticism. Most of the time, these talks are not spoken out loud. Instead, they're spoken by the mind.

A good example of this is when you see a friend of yours on the internet as you're scrolling through Facebook. You haven't seen this friend for many years, and now he's suddenly successful and driving an exotic car. On the other hand, you're doing well but have yet to get a car for yourself. Immediately, your mind begins to ask you things like, "When are you ever going to be comfortable like this?" "This guy now has a car?" "Just imagine how you've been wasting your life." "You can never get such a car with your current salary."

This negative self-talk can make you focus more on your shortcomings than on what you've achieved, making you feel inferior to those who have what you don't have. Over time, this negative self-talk can leave you feeling hurt and hopeless, despite your successes and achievements.

STRATEGIES TO BREAK THE CYCLE OF OVER-COMPARING AND COMPETING

STRATEGY 1: Limit social media use (and focus on positive and uplifting content)

Limiting social media use is useful in overcoming over-comparison and self-doubt because social media can be a breeding ground for both. Social media often portray idealized versions of people's lives, which can lead to feelings of inadequacy and self-doubt when comparing oneself to others.

By limiting your social media use, you can create space for yourself to focus on your own thoughts, goals, and desires without being constantly bombarded by comparisons to others. This can help you develop a more positive self-image and reduce over-comparisons and self-doubt.

Moreover, when you do use social media, it's essential to be mindful of the content you consume. Follow accounts that inspire and motivate you rather than those that make you feel inferior or inadequate. By doing this, you can use social media as a tool for self-improvement and personal growth, rather than as a source of negativity and self-doubt.

Limiting social media use can also help you live more in the present moment and appreciate what is going on around you. Instead of constantly comparing yourself to others and worrying about what you're missing out on, you can focus on your own life and find contentment in the present.

NOTE: It is true that we cannot entirely control what we see on social media. In this case, when you accidentally bump into any content, such as a friend's achievement, that might make you engage in self-doubt and competition, immediately think about your own achievements and the areas you're making progress in. Even when you don't have a substantial achievement yet, say to yourself, "I am following the right path, and soon enough, I will have my own ___." Fill in the gap with anything that you lack at the moment of thought.

STRATEGY 2: Recognize your strengths

When you focus on your strengths, you become less preoccupied with comparing yourself to others and more focused on what you are good at. This can help shift your mindset from one of competition to one of collaboration, where you can recognize and appreciate the strengths of others while also acknowledging your own.

Recognizing your strengths can also help to build your self-confidence and reduce self-doubt. When you have a clear understanding of what you are good at and what makes you unique, you can approach challenges and opportunities with more confidence and less anxiety. This can help you achieve your goals and reach your full potential.

Also, recognizing your strengths and accomplishments can help cultivate a more positive self-image. Instead of constantly focusing on your weaknesses and comparing yourself to others, you can appreciate your strengths and accomplishments. This can lead to a greater sense of self-worth and a more positive outlook on life.

STRATEGY 3: Reframe your thinking

This strategy is synonymous with strategy two, but a little more diverse.

It's important to recognize that comparison is a natural tendency, and it's not always easy to simply stop comparing yourself to others. Instead, you can try to change the way you think about the comparison.

One way to reframe your thinking is to focus on your own progress and accomplishments rather than comparing yourself to others. For example, if you find yourself comparing your work to that of a colleague, instead of focusing on what your colleague is doing better than you, focus on the progress you've made in your own work.

Another way to reframe your thinking is to recognize that everyone has their own unique journey and circumstances. It's not fair to compare yourself to someone else who may have had different opportunities or challenges than you. Instead, focus on what you can do with the resources and circumstances you have.

Additionally, it can be helpful to remember that everyone has their own strengths and weaknesses. Just because someone may excel in an area where you struggle, it doesn't mean they are better overall. Everyone has their own unique set of talents and abilities, and it's important to recognize and appreciate your own strengths.

To reframe your thinking and recognize your own strength, say a few words to yourself to lift your spirit:

"I am doing the best I can with the resources and circumstances I have."

"I am proud of my progress and accomplishments."

These are a positive set of affirmations that can help reframe negative thoughts and overcome comparison, competition, and self-doubt. This affirmation focuses on recognizing and accepting that you are doing the best you can with what you have, rather than comparing yourself to others or setting unrealistic expectations.

The first affirmation, "I am doing the best I can with the resources and circumstances I have," acknowledges that you are not in control of everything that happens in your life. There may be limitations, challenges, or obstacles that make it difficult to achieve your goals or compare yourself to others. By recognizing that you are doing the best you can with what you have, you can release yourself from the pressure of perfectionism and competition.

The second affirmation, "I am proud of my progress and accomplishments," focuses on celebrating your achievements and recognizing your worth and value. It's important to acknowledge your progress and accomplishments, no matter how small they may seem, and be proud of what you have achieved. By celebrating your achievements, you can boost your self-esteem and feel more confident in yourself and your abilities.

"I am unique and have my own strengths and abilities."
"I don't need to compare myself to others to feel good about myself."

These are another positive set of affirmations to help you overcome comparison and competition.

The first affirmation, "I am unique and have my own strengths and abilities," acknowledges that everyone is different and has their own unique qualities and talents. By recognizing and celebrating your strengths and abilities, you can improve your self-esteem and feel more self-assured.

The second affirmation, "I don't need to compare myself to others to feel good about myself," encourages you to focus on your own journey and progress rather than comparing yourself to others. It's easy to fall into the trap of comparing yourself to others, especially with the rise of social media and constant exposure to other people's lives. However, comparing yourself to others can lead to negative self-talk, self-doubt, and feelings of inadequacy. By focusing on your own journey and progress, you can improve your self-esteem and feel more empowered.

"Success is not a competition."
"I can achieve success in my own way and on my own terms."

These affirmations emphasize that success is not a competition and that you can define and achieve success in your own way.

The first affirmation, "Success is not a competition," acknowledges that success is not a race to the top or an opportunity to compare yourself to others. Often, we feel pressure to measure up to others' standards of success, but this can lead to negative self-talk and self-doubt. By recognizing that success is not a competition, you can release yourself from the pressure to compare yourself to others and focus on your own journey.

The second affirmation, "I can achieve success in my own way and on my own terms," emphasizes that you can define and achieve success in a way that is meaningful and fulfilling to you. Success means different things to different people, and it's important to define success in a way that aligns with your values, goals, and passions. By defining success on your terms, you can feel more empowered and motivated to pursue your own path to success.

STRATEGY 4: Compete with yourself

This strategy works for me 100% of the time. One way to compete with yourself is by setting achievable goals and striving to improve yourself every day.

Instead of comparing yourself to others and trying to outdo them, you focus on your own progress and aim to be better than you were yesterday. This strategy helps you stop comparing yourself to others and competing with them by shifting your focus from external validation to internal motivation.

When you compete with yourself, you set goals that are tailored to your own strengths, weaknesses, and aspirations. You identify what you want to achieve and create a plan to get there. This process allows you to set realistic goals and develop a sense of purpose and direction. By focusing on your progress and success, you become less preoccupied with comparing yourself to others and more focused on your journey.

In addition, competing with yourself can help you build self-confidence and reduce self-doubt. When you set achievable goals and make progress towards them, you gain a sense of accomplishment and a belief in your own abilities. This can help you to feel more confident in your skin and less concerned with what others are doing.

STRATEGY 5: Be grateful

This strategy helps you shift your focus from what you don't have to what you do have.

When you cultivate a sense of gratitude, you become more aware of the positive aspects of your life and less preoccupied with what others have that you don't.

Being grateful involves focusing on the present moment and acknowledging the good things in your life. This could be as simple as appreciating a beautiful sunset, a kind gesture from a friend, or a warm meal. When you focus on the positive aspects of your life, you become less preoccupied with what others have and more content with what you have.

Moreover, being grateful can help you develop a more positive mindset and reduce feelings of inadequacy and self-doubt. When you cultivate a sense of gratitude, you become more aware of the good things in your life and less concerned with what others have. This can lead to a greater sense of contentment and fulfillment, which can help you avoid over-comparing and competing with others.

Finally, being grateful can help you develop a more positive outlook on life. By focusing on the positive aspects of your life, you become more resilient in the face of challenges and setbacks. This can help you overcome obstacles and achieve your goals with greater ease and confidence.

Below are some positive affirmations to help you express and teach yourself the spirit of gratitude.

"I am grateful for all the blessings in my life."

This is an affirmation that expresses gratitude for the positive things in one's life. By focusing on the blessings, you acknowledge the good things you have and cultivate a positive outlook. This affirmation can help you overcome over-comparing and competing with others by shifting the focus away from what you lack, towards what you have. It can also help to reduce feelings of inadequacy and self-doubt by reminding you of the good things in your life. Overall, expressing gratitude through affirmations like this one can promote a sense of contentment, fulfillment, and joy in life.

"I am grateful for my unique talents and abilities."

"I am grateful for my unique talents and abilities" is an affirmation that expresses gratitude for the skills and qualities that make you who you are. By focusing on your unique talents and abilities, you acknowledge your strengths and cultivate a positive self-image. This affirmation can help you overcome over-comparing and competing with others by reminding you that you have your own unique set of strengths and skills that no one else possesses. It can also help reduce feelings of inadequacy and self-doubt by reminding you that you have valuable qualities that contribute to the world in your own unique way. Lastly, expressing gratitude for your unique talents and abilities through affirmations like this one can instill confidence, self-acceptance, and fulfillment.

"I am grateful for the opportunities that come my way."

There is no better way to express gratitude for the chance to grow and improve in life than this affirmation does.

By focusing on the opportunities, you acknowledge that life is full of possibilities and that you have the power to make the most of them. This affirmation can help you overcome over-comparing and competing with others by reminding you that everyone has their own unique path in life and that the opportunities you receive are part of your journey. It can also help to reduce feelings of inadequacy and self-doubt by reminding you that every opportunity is a chance to learn and grow, no matter the outcome. In addition, expressing gratitude for the opportunities that come your way through affirmations like this one can pave the way for optimism, resilience, and gratitude for the journey of life.

"I am grateful for the abundance in my life."

Focusing on gratitude for the abundance in your life is a powerful strategy to overcome the negative effects of over-comparing and competing with others. When you express gratitude for what you have, you shift your focus from what you lack to what you already possess, and this can help you feel more content and satisfied with your life.

When you constantly compare yourself to others, you may fall into the trap of feeling like you never have enough or that you are not good enough. This can lead to feelings of inadequacy, envy, and even depression. By cultivating a mindset of abundance and gratitude, you can break this cycle of negativity and find more joy in your life.

"I am grateful for the simple pleasures that bring me joy."

Expressing gratitude for the simple pleasures that bring you joy can help you overcome over-comparing and competing by shifting your focus from external measures of success or achievement to the present moment and the things that bring you happiness. By appreciating the small, everyday things that make you happy, you can find contentment and joy within yourself rather than seeking validation or satisfaction from external sources. This can help you break free from the cycle of comparing yourself to others and competing for external rewards. Instead, you'll be able to focus on what truly matters to you.

"I am grateful for the journey of self-discovery and growth."

When you are grateful for your own journey, you become more focused on your unique path and less concerned with comparing yourself to others or competing with them. This can help you cultivate a more positive and self-affirming mindset, which can boost your confidence and self-worth. It can also help you appreciate the lessons you learn along the way, even when they are challenging, by viewing them as opportunities for growth rather than failures or setbacks. Ultimately, this gratitude can help you stay grounded and centered in your journey, allowing you to reach your full potential without being held back by comparisons or competition with others.

REMEMBER: There is no faster way to kill your self-confidence and self-belief than over-comparing and competing. No matter what you've achieved in life, there is always someone somewhere better than you. All you need to do is appreciate what you've achieved and be content with what you have.

Key Takeaways

With the strategies and tips we have discussed in this chapter, we have been able to learn the following:

- What it means to compare and compete
- Consequences of over-comparing and competing
- The comparison and competing mentality and how it relates to self-doubt
- How to catch yourself comparing and competing
- How to break the cycle of over-comparing and competing

In the next chapter, we are going to find out what defines your self-image. Are you the one giving others permission to define your self-image? Are you the one responsible for how you see yourself as well as how others see you? Well, let's find out in the next chapter!

CHAPTER 4

YOU'RE GIVING THEM PERMISSION

"It's hard to feel desire when you don't feel desirable."
— Christine Feehan

When you give people permission and circumstances to create and define your self-image, you are essentially allowing them to have control over how you see yourself. This can happen when you seek validation, acceptance, or approval from others, and in doing so, you give them the power to shape your sense of self. While this might seem harmless at first, it can later lead to self-doubt, as you may start questioning whether your self-image is truly yours or the product of external influences.

To better illustrate this, let's consider this example. Imagine you are a young woman who has always struggled with body image issues. You constantly compare yourself to others, especially those with "perfect" bodies. You allow social media, magazines, and TV shows to define what is beautiful and desirable, and you feel pressured to conform to these unrealistic standards. As a result, you've rejected your own unique look that was only meant for you and given to you to continue to define it.

Now let's consider a different scenario. Imagine that you are a student who has always been passionate about music. You love playing the piano, writing songs, and performing in front of others. However, your parents might not see any potential in your skills or talent. They urge you to study something more practical, like business or engineering. You feel torn between your love for music and your desire to please your parents. You begin to doubt your abilities and talents, and you wonder if you will ever be good enough to make it in the music industry.

In both examples, the individuals allow external factors to shape their self-image. They are giving others permission to define what is beautiful, desirable, and successful. This can lead to a lack of self-confidence and cause them to disconnect from their true selves. Over time, this can cause them to question their worth and capabilities, which can lead to self-doubt and a lack of motivation.

Furthermore, the problem with allowing others to create and define our self-image is that it can be very subjective and arbitrary. What one person considers beautiful, another person may find unattractive. What one person considers successful, another person may view as a failure. By relying on external sources to define our self-worth, we are essentially putting our fate in the hands of others who may not have our best interests at heart.

For instance, consider the fashion industry, which has long been criticized for perpetuating unrealistic beauty standards and promoting unhealthy body ideals. Models are often expected to conform to a certain body type and size, and those who don't fit this mold are often excluded from the industry. This can be very damaging to the self-esteem of young women who aspire to be models, as they may feel that they are not good enough or pretty enough to succeed in this field.

Another example is the pressure that young people face to excel academically and professionally. Students are often told that they need to get good grades, attend prestigious universities, and land high-paying jobs in order to be successful. This can create a sense of competition and comparison, which can lead to self-doubt and anxiety. Students may feel that they are not smart enough or talented enough to meet these expectations, which can cause them to feel hopeless.

WHY YOU SHOULDN'T ALLOW OTHER PEOPLE'S INSECURITIES TO CREATE YOUR SELF-IMAGE

Allowing other people's insecurities to create your self-image is harmful. Here are some of the main reasons why you shouldn't let this happen:

It can limit your potential

Allowing other people's insecurities to shape your self-image can have a significant impact on your potential. When you start considering other people's insecurities as your own, you internalize their limitations and negative beliefs about yourself. This can lead to a negative self-image and a lack of confidence in your own abilities and potential.

By adopting other people's insecurities and limitations, you essentially become them and allow them to shape your identity and actions. You may start to limit yourself in the same ways they do, or you may begin to see yourself as incapable or unworthy.

This can be a very damaging pattern, as it prevents you from fully exploring your potential and living a fulfilling life.

Also, internalizing negative opinions or criticisms from others can create self-doubt and limit your belief in your abilities. This can also prevent you from taking risks, pursuing your goals, and reaching your full potential.

For example, imagine that you're interested in pursuing a career in a field that your parents disapprove of. They may tell you that the field is not lucrative, or that you're not cut out for it. If you allow their opinions to shape your self-image, you may start to believe that you're not capable of succeeding in that field. This can limit your potential and prevent you from pursuing a career that you're passionate about.

Another example is in sports or athletics. If you allow negative feedback or criticisms from a coach or teammates to shape your self-image, it can limit your potential as an athlete. You may start to second guess your abilities and shy away from taking risks or trying new techniques, thus preventing you from improving and reaching your full potential in your sport.

Moreover, in academic or intellectual pursuits, if you allow negative comments or criticism from peers or professors to shape your self-image, it can limit your potential to achieve academic excellence. You may start to believe that you're not smart enough or capable enough to succeed, which can prevent you from putting in the effort needed to excel in your studies.

Additionally, in the workplace, if you allow negative feedback or criticism from your boss or coworkers to shape your self-image, it can limit your potential for career advancement. You may start to believe that you're incapable of taking on new responsibilities or challenges, which can prevent you from pursuing promotions or seeking new opportunities.

In all of these scenarios, allowing other people's insecurities to shape your self-image can limit your potential in various ways. It's important to recognize that other people's opinions and criticisms are not a reflection of your true potential and that you have the power to define your own abilities and goals.

It can cause you to ignore your own needs

When you allow other people's insecurities to shape your self-image, you may start to prioritize their needs and expectations over your own. This can lead to a situation where you're constantly trying to please others at the expense of your own needs and desires. Over time, this can lead to frustration, burnout, and even resentment.

Let's say that you have a friend who is very critical of your appearance. They may make comments about your clothing, hair, or makeup and make you feel self-conscious. If you allow their insecurities to shape your self-image, you may start to prioritize their opinions over your own. This could lead you to dress or style yourself in a way that pleases them rather than expressing your own sense of style or comfort.

To corroborate this, let's use another example. Let's assume you're in a romantic relationship. If you allow your partner's insecurities to shape your self-image, you may start to prioritize their needs and expectations over your own. This manifests when you give up hobbies or interests that you enjoy in order to spend more time with your partner or to avoid conflict. This can lead to a situation where you're not meeting your own needs or pursuing your own goals, which can be detrimental to your happiness and well-being.

Also, in the workplace, if you allow other people's insecurities to shape your self-image, you may start to prioritize their needs and expectations over your own. For instance, you may take on extra work or responsibilities in order to impress your boss or avoid criticism from coworkers. As a result, you fail to tend to your own needs, such as getting enough rest or maintaining a healthy work-life balance.

In addition, this is also possible in friendships. Obviously, when you agree to plans or activities that you're not interested in, simply to avoid disappointing your friend or to fit in with their social circle, you're ignoring your own needs while falling prey to their needs and desires. Ultimately, you may find that you're neglecting your needs, when you're unable to pursue your interests or spend time alone.

It can lead to conformity

This is a psychological effect that allows other people's insecurities to create your self-image. Even without realizing it, you find yourself not expressing your true self or pursuing your own goals, but instead trying to fit in with the expectations of others. Over time, it can lead to dissatisfaction or even a loss of identity.

Imagine that you're part of a group of friends who have a particular set of beliefs or values. If you allow their insecurities to shape your self-image, you may start to conform to their expectations in order to fit in. This could mean adopting their beliefs or values, even if they don't align with your own. This can lead to a situation where you're not expressing your true self but instead trying to fit in with the expectations of others.

Another expression of this is in the workplace. In the workplace, you may start to adopt the same work style or approach as your coworkers, even if it doesn't align with your own strengths or preferences. This can lead to you not expressing your own unique abilities or pursuing your own career goals but instead being influenced by others' expectations, styles, and approaches.

NOTE: When you allow other people's insecurities to dictate your self-image, you're essentially giving them power over your thoughts and emotions. This can be especially harmful if you're already prone to self-doubt or have low self-esteem.

WHAT A GOOD SELF-IMAGE ENTAILS

Having a good self-image is an essential component of a healthy and fulfilling life. A good self-image means having a positive and accurate perception of oneself, as well as accepting and valuing oneself. It involves recognizing one's strengths and weaknesses, and having a realistic view of oneself that is not distorted by negative self-talk or societal pressures.

A good self-image also involves self-care, self-love, and self-respect. It means treating oneself with kindness, compassion, and respect, and taking care of one's physical, emotional, and mental well-being. This includes engaging in activities that promote health and well-being, such as exercise, healthy eating, meditation, and getting enough sleep.

Furthermore, a good self-image means being comfortable with oneself and expressing oneself authentically. This involves being true to oneself, expressing oneself in a way that feels genuine and authentic, and not conforming to the expectations of others. It also involves having healthy boundaries, being able to communicate effectively, and maintaining healthy relationships with others.

A good self-image is not something that is achieved overnight. It takes time and effort to develop a positive self-image, especially if one has experienced negative messages about oneself in the past.

5 Unique Food for Thought

1. Having others define your self-image is basically you trying to become what they wish they were

When you allow others to define your self-image, you are allowing them to shape your identity and self-worth. Essentially, you are taking on their expectations, desires, and values as your own. This can lead you to become a version of yourself that is not true to who you really are, but rather, a reflection of what others want you to be.

When you seek validation from others and base your self-worth on their opinions of you, you are essentially trying to become what they wish they were. You are trying to fit into their expectations and ideals, rather than staying true to your own unique sense of self. This can cause you to feel insecure and unhappy since you are not living authentically.

For example, if someone constantly receives praise for their academic achievements, they may feel pressure to continue performing at a high level in order to maintain that positive self-image. This can lead to them sacrificing other aspects of their lives, such as hobbies or social relationships, in order to focus solely on their academics. They may also feel they cannot deviate from this path, as doing so would risk losing the validation they receive from others.

Furthermore, if your self-image is based on the opinions of others, you may constantly seek external validation and approval rather than being self-sufficient and confident in your abilities. This can lead to a cycle of dependency, where you are constantly seeking the approval of others and neglecting your own needs and desires.

2. *Becoming another's self-image = being a second version of them = you'll always be second best*

When we become another's self-image, we are essentially becoming a version of them. We are molding ourselves to fit their expectations and desires, rather than staying true to our own unique sense of self. This can cause us to lose our sense of identity and individuality and make us feel like we are living in someone else's shadow.

When we are living as the second version of someone else, we may always feel like we are second best. We are essentially living in their shadow and may struggle to establish our own sense of worth and identity. We may feel like we are not living up to our full potential and may be at risk of losing our sense of self.

For example, if someone's self-image is based on the expectations of their parents, they may feel like they are living in their parent's shadow, constantly striving to meet their expectations and desires. They may feel like they can never measure up to their parents' achievements or live up to their expectations, which can lead to feelings of inadequacy and self-doubt.

3. Everyone will fail to be you, because no one has the gifts and talent to be you. You hold the secret to you, and it's your job to go find out

Every individual is unique and possesses a set of qualities, talents, and gifts that are distinct from others. No two individuals are exactly alike, and it is important to recognize and embrace our unique attributes.

When you try to be someone else or allow others to define your sense of self, you essentially deny your individuality and the things that set you apart. It is important to acknowledge that you hold the secret to who you are, and that it is your responsibility to discover and embrace your individuality.

No one else can be you or possess the same abilities that you do. You must recognize and embrace your unique qualities and talents and use them to your advantage. This will allow you to discover your true passions, interests, and goals and find fulfillment and purpose in your life.

For example, if someone is passionate about music, they may have a unique talent for playing a particular instrument or composing music. This talent is unique to them, and no one else can replicate it in the same way. By recognizing and embracing this talent, they can pursue their passion for music and find fulfillment in their lives.

In essence, you must embrace what is unique to you, rather than try to be someone else or allow others to define your sense of self. You hold the secret to who you are, and it is your responsibility to discover and embrace your individuality. By doing so, you can find fulfillment and purpose in your life, and make a positive impact on the world around you.

4. *Who you wish to be (realistically not like having superpowers or becoming a superhero etc.) gives you a glimpse of your true self*

The person that we wish to be is often a reflection of our true selves, our aspirations, and our values. When envisioning who we want to be, we are essentially tapping into our own inner desires, hopes, and dreams.

Our true selves are often obscured by external influences, such as societal expectations, family pressure, or peer pressure. We may feel that we need to conform to these external expectations in order to fit in or be accepted, and in doing so, we may lose sight of our true selves.

However, when we imagine who we want to be, we are often able to tap into our innermost desires and aspirations and connect with our true selves. This can help us to identify the values that are most important to us and to create a vision for our future that aligns with our own unique aspirations.

For example, if someone wishes to be a successful entrepreneur, they may be tapping into their own desire for independence, creativity, and financial freedom. By envisioning themselves as a successful entrepreneur, they may be uncovering their true aspirations and values.

In essence, when we imagine who we want to be, we are often seeing a glimpse of who we really are. We are tapping into our innermost desires and aspirations, and by embracing this vision of our future, we can begin to take steps toward realizing our true potential and creating a life that is aligned with our own unique aspirations.

5. What you see only requires development

When we observe something, whether it be a skill, an idea, or a talent, we may be inclined to believe this is something that is inherent or innate. However, in many cases, what we see only requires development and can be learned and honed through practice and dedication.

For example, if someone observes a skilled athlete performing at a high level, they may believe that the athlete possesses a natural talent or ability that cannot be learned or developed. However, in reality, the athlete has likely dedicated countless hours to training, practicing, and perfecting their craft, which has allowed them to develop their skills and abilities to a high level.

Similarly, if someone observes a successful entrepreneur, they may believe that the entrepreneur has a unique set of skills or talents that cannot be learned or developed. However, the entrepreneur has likely worked hard to develop their skills and knowledge through education, mentorship, and experience.

In essence, what we see only requires development, and many of the skills and abilities we admire in others can be learned and honed through practice and dedication. We may need to put in the time and effort to develop our skills and abilities, but with persistence and hard work, we can achieve our goals and realize our full potential.

By recognizing that what we see only requires development, we can become more confident in our abilities and less intimidated by the accomplishments of others. We can focus on developing our own skills and knowledge, and work towards realizing our goals and aspirations.

Key Takeaways

We have been able to look at what it means to give people permission to create your self-image for you. In addition, we learned the following:

- Why you shouldn't allow other people's insecurities to create your self-image
- What a good self-image entails

Now that we've equipped ourselves with a clear view of what a good self-image entails, let's now look at where self-doubt actually arises from. Does it arise from your reaction or how people in our lives react to our mistakes? Well, we will find out in the next chapter!

The Truth About Self-Doubt

CHAPTER 5

THEY'RE ONLY REACTIONS, NOT THE TRUTH!

"Believe in yourself, your abilities, and your own potential. Never let self-doubt hold you captive. You are worthy of all that you dream of and hope for."

— Roy Bennett

When people make comments or judgments about us, it is important to remember that these are simply *their* reactions or opinions; they do not necessarily reflect the truth about us or our worth. Our true worth is determined by our inherent value as human beings, which cannot be changed or defined by external factors such as other people's opinions or judgments.

It is natural to feel hurt or defensive when others make negative comments or judgments about us, but it is important to recognize that their opinions are just that - opinions. They may be based on limited information, biases, or their own personal issues and do not necessarily reflect who we are as individuals.

Ultimately, we have the power to define our own worth and to choose how we respond to other people's comments or judgments. By focusing on our values, strengths, and abilities, and refusing to let other people's opinions define us, we can cultivate a more positive and empowered sense of self.

DO NOT FORGET: One of the challenges of dealing with self-doubt is that we cannot control the reactions of others. We may encounter people who are negative or critical, and it can be difficult to avoid their influence.

However, we can take steps to manage our own reactions to their behavior and cultivate a stronger sense of self-worth and confidence.

STRATEGIES TO DISCERN EVERY RESPONSE CORRECTLY

It can be challenging to completely avoid being affected by other people's reactions, but there are some practical strategies you can use to help you discern and interpret them in a more positive and constructive way. Below are a few strategies:

STRATEGY 1: Consider the source

"Consider the source" means that before taking any action or making a decision, it's important to evaluate the credibility of the person providing the information or feedback. This can be especially important when it comes to evaluating negative feedback or criticism from others. In this context, "consider the source" means that you should take into account the person's background, expertise, and motivations before giving their feedback or criticism much weight.

When you "consider the source," you can more accurately assess the validity of the feedback or criticism you receive. For example, if a coworker who has a history of being unreliable gives you negative feedback on a project, you may not take it as seriously as you would if the feedback came from someone who is known to be competent and dependable. In this case, you are

91

considering the source to determine whether the feedback is reliable or not.

Considering the source can also be useful when evaluating feedback or criticism that may be biased or unfair. For example, if you are a person of color and receive negative feedback from someone who has a history of racist comments or behavior, you may be more likely to dismiss the feedback as biased and invalid. Going through this process helps to ascertain whether the feedback is fair and objective.

When considering the source, it's important to take into account several factors, including:

Expertise: Is the person providing the feedback or criticism an expert on the subject matter? If so, their feedback may be more valuable than someone who lacks expertise.

Objectivity: Is the person providing the feedback or criticism objective, or do they have a vested interest in the outcome? For example, if a competitor provides negative feedback on your business, their feedback may be biased.

Motivations: Why is the person providing the feedback or criticism? Are they trying to help you improve, or are they trying to tear you down? Understanding their motivations can help you evaluate the validity of their feedback.

Reputation: What is the person's reputation in your industry or community? Do they have a history of providing reliable feedback, or are they known for being unreliable or biased?

Relationship: What is your relationship with the person providing the feedback or criticism? Are they a friend, coworkers, or someone you barely know? Your relationship with the person can impact how you perceive their feedback.

For example, let's say you're a new employee at a company, and your supervisor provides you with negative feedback on a project you worked on. If your supervisor has a reputation for being a fair and objective evaluator, you may be more likely to take the feedback seriously and use it to improve your performance. On the other hand, if your supervisor has a history of playing favorites or providing unfair feedback, you may be more likely to dismiss the feedback as biased or irrelevant.

Another example is in the context of social media. When receiving negative comments on social media, it's important to consider the source before taking the criticism to heart. Often, people who leave negative comments on social media do so anonymously or without considering the impact of their words. If the person leaving negative comments has a history of trolling or harassing others, it's likely that their feedback is not coming from a place of constructive criticism.

NOTE: If the person providing the negative feedback has a reputable history, it doesn't mean you should doubt yourself or your ability to be successful in that very area that caused the negative feedback.

Instead, keep calm and see the comment as an opportunity for growth and improvement. Even if the feedback is difficult to hear, it's important to remember that constructive criticism can help us improve our skills and performance.

Here are some steps you can take when receiving negative feedback from a reputable source in order to not succumb to self-doubt:

Step 1: Listen actively

When receiving feedback, it's important to listen actively to what the other person is saying. Avoid getting defensive or dismissive, and instead, try to understand their perspective.

Step 2: Ask questions

If you're unsure about the feedback you've received, ask the person for more information or clarification. This can help you better understand their perspective and use the feedback to improve your performance.

Step 3: Don't take it personally

It's natural to feel defensive or hurt when receiving negative feedback, but it's important not to take it personally. Remember that the feedback is about your performance, not about you as a person.

We will go more in details on this in the next strategy.

Step 4: Reflect on the feedback

Take some time to reflect on the feedback you've received. Think about how you can use the feedback to improve your skills or performance.

Step 5: Develop an action plan

Once you've reflected on the feedback, develop an action plan to improve your skills or performance. Set specific, measurable goals for yourself and create a timeline for achieving them.

Step 6: Follow up

Once you've implemented your action plan, follow up with the person who provided the feedback. Let them know what steps you've taken to improve, and ask for their feedback on your progress.

REMEMBER: By taking these steps, you can use negative feedback from a reputable source to improve your skills and performance instead of allowing it to get to you and cause self-doubt. Remember, constructive criticism is a valuable tool for growth and development. Even negative feedback can help us become better versions of ourselves.

STRATEGY 2: Don't take things personally

What does it mean to take things personally? This implies three solid remarks:

It shows a victim mentality

Taking things personally shows a victim mentality, where the whole world is out to get and destroy you. When someone takes things personally, they often assume that other people's actions or words are directed at them, and they interpret them as a reflection of their worth or identity. This can lead to feelings of hurt, anger, or defensiveness, as well as a tendency to take things out of context or blow them out of proportion. When this pattern becomes chronic or pervasive, it can indicate a victim mentality, where the person sees themselves as constantly under attack or being treated unfairly. Believing this creates a sense of powerlessness, as well as a tendency to blame others for their problems or shortcomings. The belief that the world is out to get them and destroy them is a hallmark of a victim mentality. This mindset can prevent people from taking responsibility for their actions and choices, and it can also prevent them from seeking help or support when they need it.

It makes you live your life through a false filter, seeing people as only attacking you

This is similar to the point above. When you take things personally, you begin to feel that every comment people make about you, whether genuine or not, is an attack. This thought can prevent you from personal development as your attitude or response toward their comment would become a defensive one, instead of being one of humility and willingness to learn from your mistakes.

It shows you're still nurturing your internal pain and have not dealt with it

When someone takes things personally, such as comments or judgments about their actions, it can indicate that they have unresolved internal pain or emotional wounds that are still affecting them. By taking such comments or judgments as personal attacks, they may be inadvertently reopening these wounds and experiencing the pain again. If someone has truly dealt with their internal pain, they are more likely to respond to comments or judgments in a more objective and detached manner, recognizing that other people's opinions do not define them. They are less likely to feel personally attacked or offended because they have already worked through their internal issues and are secure in their own sense of self-worth.

NOTE: When we take things personally, we tend to internalize negative comments or feedback and view them as a reflection of our own self-worth. This can lead to feelings of self-doubt and low self-esteem. On the other hand, when we don't take things personally, we are better able to separate our sense of self from external opinions and feedback.

For example, let's say that you've received some negative feedback on a project you've been working on. If you take the feedback personally, you might start to doubt your abilities and feel like a failure. This could lead to a negative spiral of self-doubt and self-criticism, making it harder to make progress on the project.

However, if you don't take the feedback personally, you can view it as an opportunity to learn and grow. You can ask questions and seek clarification rather than assuming that the feedback means you're a bad person or a failure. This can help you avoid self-doubt and instead focus on using the feedback to improve your work.

Another example might be if you receive a negative comment or judgment from someone in your personal life. If you take the comment personally, you might feel hurt and defensive, leading to arguments and strained relationships. However, if you don't take the comment personally, you can view it as a difference of opinion or perspective rather than a personal attack. This can help you avoid uncertainty and instead allows you to focus on maintaining positive relationships with the people in your life.

In general, not taking things personally can help you avoid self-doubt by allowing you to view feedback and comments from others as external to yourself. This can help you maintain your confidence and self-worth, even in the face of negative feedback or criticism. It can also help you avoid getting caught up in negative thought patterns or self-criticism, allowing you to stay focused on your goals and objectives.

STRATEGY 3: Challenge your thoughts on the comment that is causing you to take it personally

Challenging your thoughts on a comment that causes you to take it personally is an important technique for overcoming the effects of negative feedback, comments, and judgments from others. When we receive negative feedback, our thoughts and emotions can quickly spiral into negativity and self-doubt. By challenging these negative thoughts, we can take a more balanced and objective view of the situation and avoid getting caught up in unhealthy thought patterns.

For example, let's say that you've received negative feedback on a presentation you gave at work. You might initially doubt yourself or resort to negativity, which may cause you to believe you're not a good presenter and that you'll never improve. By challenging these thoughts, you can ask yourself if they're really true. Is there evidence to support them, or are they based on fear or assumption? You might also look for evidence to the contrary, such as positive feedback you've received in the past or improvements you've made since your last presentation. By practicing positive self-talk and taking action to improve your presentation skills, you can overcome the negative effects of the feedback and build confidence in your abilities.

Below are a few things you can do to challenge your thoughts:

Step 1: First, identify the thoughts that are causing you to take unfavorable feedback personally

To challenge the thoughts causing you to take unfavorable feedback personally, it's important to first identify them. These thoughts are often automatic and can be difficult to recognize, so paying close attention to your pattern of thinking and emotions in response to negative feedback, comments, or judgments from others can be helpful.

One way to identify these thoughts is to pay attention to your self-talk. Self-talk is the internal dialogue we have with ourselves throughout the day, and it can be positive or negative. It might include thoughts like "I'm not good enough," "I'll never be able to do this," or "Everyone thinks I'm a failure." When you notice negative self-talk, take a moment to pause and reflect on the thought.

Another way to identify these thoughts is to pay attention to your emotions. Negative feedback, comments, or judgments from others can trigger a range of negative emotions, such as anger, sadness, or anxiety. These emotions can signal that you're having negative thoughts and can help you identify them.

Finally, it can be helpful to keep a journal of your thoughts and emotions. Writing down your thoughts and emotions can help you identify negative thinking patterns and recognize triggers that lead to self-doubt.

By identifying negative thoughts, you can take steps to challenge them and reframe them in a more positive or realistic way. This can help you overcome self-doubt and build confidence in your abilities.

Step 2: Challenge the comment-induced thought that is making you take it personally

Once you've identified the thought caused by people's comments or judgments from others, the next step is to challenge it. Challenging the thought involves questioning the validity and accuracy of the thought and looking for evidence to support or refute it.

To challenge the comment-induced thought, you can ask yourself a series of questions, such as:

Is the thought based on fact or assumption?

Often, thoughts caused by bad comments or judgment are based more on assumptions or fears than actual evidence. By questioning the validity of the thought, you can begin to challenge its accuracy.

Is the thought helpful or harmful?

Comment-induced thoughts that make us take it personally can be harmful to our self-esteem and confidence. By recognizing the negative effects of the thought, you can challenge it and replace it with a more positive or realistic one.

What evidence supports this thought?

Look for evidence to support or refute this thought. If there is evidence to support it, consider how you might address the situation to improve the outcome. If there is no evidence to support it, consider how you might reframe the thought in a more positive or realistic way.

What would you say to a friend in a similar situation?

Sometimes, we are more compassionate and understanding toward our friends than we are toward ourselves. By imagining what you would say to a friend in a similar situation, you can challenge comment-induced thoughts and offer yourself more compassion and support.

NOTE: By challenging these thoughts, you can begin to break the cycle of self-doubt and negativity. It can be helpful to practice this technique regularly, as these thoughts can be persistent and difficult to overcome. Over time, with practice, you can develop a more positive and resilient mindset and build confidence in your abilities.

Step 3: Look for evidence to the contrary

When challenging thoughts that sprout from people's judgments, feedback, and comments about you, it can be helpful to look for evidence to the contrary. This means actively seeking examples and experiences that contradict the thought and using them to challenge its validity.

For example, if you receive negative feedback on a project at work and start to think, "I'm not good at my job," you can look for evidence to the contrary. This might involve thinking about past successes and accomplishments at work or seeking positive feedback from colleagues or supervisors. By focusing on evidence that contradicts the thought, you can challenge its validity and build confidence in your abilities.

Looking for evidence to the contrary can also involve challenging black-and-white thinking. Comments that are taken personally often involve all-or-nothing thinking, where we see things as either completely positive or completely negative. By looking for evidence that falls in between these extremes, we can counteract these thoughts and develop a more balanced perspective.

For example, if you receive a negative comment on a social media post and start to think, "I'm a terrible writer," you can look for evidence to the contrary. This might involve thinking about past positive comments on your writing or seeking constructive feedback from a trusted friend or mentor. By acknowledging the areas where you can improve while also recognizing your strengths, you can challenge your thoughts and build confidence in your abilities.

Looking for evidence to the contrary can be a powerful tool in overcoming self-doubt and thoughts that arise from people's comments. Although these comments may cause you to take them to heart, you can challenge their validity and develop a more positive and resilient mindset by actively identifying evidence that contradicts these thoughts.

STRATEGY 3: Set realistic expectations

Setting realistic expectations is a crucial element in avoiding self-doubt when receiving negative feedback, comments, and judgments from others. When we set unrealistic expectations for ourselves, we set ourselves up for failure, which can lead to self-doubt and a negative mindset.

By setting realistic expectations, we can avoid the negative effects of self-doubt and maintain a positive outlook on our abilities and potential. For example, if you receive negative feedback from a colleague on a narrative piece you worked on, setting realistic expectations can help you stay focused and motivated to improve.

Setting realistic expectations involves being honest with yourself about what you can accomplish and what is achievable within a certain timeframe. It's important to consider your skills, resources, and limitations when setting these expectations. Doing so allows you to create a plan that is both achievable and challenging while still allowing for growth and improvement.

For example, if you're working on a new project at work, set realistic expectations by breaking down the project into smaller, achievable tasks. This can help you stay focused and motivated while still allowing room for improvement. By setting achievable goals and expectations, you can avoid the negative effects of self-doubt and maintain a positive mindset.

Another example could be setting realistic expectations for personal goals, such as weight loss or exercise. Once you've set realistic goals that are achievable, you can avoid the uncertainty and aim to achieve a positive mindset. Setting unrealistic goals, such as losing 20 pounds in a week, can lead to frustration and self-doubt if you don't achieve them.

NOTE: In case you're finding it difficult to set realistic expectations, you can follow these quick, easy, but effective steps to do so:

Step 1: Be specific with what you desire to achieve

Being able to have a clear visualization of what you want to achieve is essential. Imagine you just finished writing a narrative piece. You saw some calls for submission to a particular journal. This submission is in different categories (poetry, fiction, and non-fiction). You're specifically good at fiction writing. However, because you're more concerned about the prize to be won than the quality of your writing, you then decide to submit to all the genres, even when you know you aren't good at the other two. Now, you have sent the writings over. You then said to yourself, "I am going to win all categories and come home with this prize." Even though you've set an expectation for yourself, it is quite an unrealistic one because you're setting your hopes too high for something you know you aren't good at. When you receive a rejection, you begin to doubt your ability, and self-doubt now creeps in. This should be avoided. To set realistic expectations, you need to be honest with yourself about your abilities. Hope for the best but prepare for the worst. Specificity means focusing on that one area you're good at and channeling all your energy into excelling in that area.

Step 2: Write down how to achieve your expectations

This step involves planning, and it is all about having a guide to help you follow your expectations. It involves threading the right path. It is only when you're following the right path that you disengage from self-doubt or overthinking. After being specific with what you want to achieve, how do you achieve them? Let's say you want to take an exam, and you expect to pass mathematics with nothing less than an A. How do you achieve this? Do you sleep throughout the night or burn the midnight candle? Map out your plan. In this case, you should find every necessary material to help you prepare for the exam. The same thing applies when going for an interview. You will need to source information about the company from people who've been there before. When you're fully prepared, your confidence level will be higher, and it could make you overcome self-doubt by feeling you have the morale needed to pass the interview.

NOTE: the good thing about mapping out your expectations is that it helps you feel like you're on track and it also equips you with a specific time frame to get the job done instead of procrastinating. Even when you fail the interview after all the preparation, you can easily look back and say, "I did my best," instead of saying, "I could have…" or "I should have…."

Step 3: Focus on the process

The old adage, "It's about the trip, not the goal," rings true in many situations. One method to maintain optimism in the face of criticism is to keep your attention on the small steps you're taking every day to move closer to your goals.

Everything will work out for the best in the end, and you should surely rejoice when it does, but you shouldn't beat yourself up over setbacks. It's important to focus on the journey toward success as much as the high you'll experience once you've reached your objective. We get hooked on the idea that achieving our goals will constitute "success." The problem is that we have no say in how things turn out, so our success is contingent on factors over which we have no control.

When you focus on the process, you don't have to listen to what people say or the terrible comments they make about you. By focusing on the process, you have something to look forward to and be hopeful about.

Step 4: Understand your why

Having a compelling "why" behind your expectations can serve as a source of continued inspiration and drive. Ask yourself these questions. Why do you want to strengthen your relationships? Why do you want to work out more? Why do you want to look for a new job?

When you're able to ask these questions, it will give you a sense of purpose. This can help you overcome self-doubt in the future and provide motivation to keep pushing.

Step 5: Reframe your mind from the "all or nothing" thinking

Another common source of self-sabotage is the 'all-or-nothing' mentality, which explains why many people abandon their objectives or resolutions so quickly. Individuals frequently adopt an all-or-nothing frame of mind, believing it is better to go all in on the cheat day than to acknowledge a minor failure before getting back on track. "All-or-nothing" thinking is the easiest to become doubtful. When you aren't flexible enough in your plan, you are already making the mistake of setting the standard too high.

STRATEGY 4: Reframe mistakes and opportunities

Reframing mistakes and opportunities is another effective strategy for avoiding self-doubt when receiving negative feedback, comments, and judgments from others. This strategy involves changing how you perceive mistakes and failures to view them as learning opportunities rather than setbacks.

When you reframe mistakes and failures as opportunities to learn and grow, you can avoid the negative effects of self-doubt and maintain a positive outlook on your abilities and potential. For example, if you receive negative feedback on a job you did, you can reframe the mistake as an opportunity to improve and learn from the feedback.

Another example could be reframing missed opportunities as chances to learn and grow. If you don't get the job you applied for, instead of feeling defeated, look at it as an opportunity to improve your skills and interview techniques for future job applications.

By reframing mistakes and opportunities, you can avoid the negative effects of self-doubt and maintain a positive mindset. This can lead to increased motivation, improved performance, and, ultimately, success. When you see mistakes and failures as opportunities to learn and grow, you are more likely to take risks and push yourself out of your comfort zone, which can lead to greater personal and professional growth.

STRATEGY 5: Practice assertiveness

Practicing assertiveness is an important step in avoiding self-doubt when receiving negative feedback, comments, and judgments from others. Assertiveness involves expressing your needs, opinions, and feelings in a clear, confident, and respectful way.

When you practice assertiveness, you can avoid the negative effects of self-doubt by taking control of the situation and standing up for yourself. For example, if someone makes a negative comment about your appearance, instead of doubting yourself or your dressing sense, you can respond assertively by calmly and respectfully explaining your perspective and defending your choice of dress.

The question is, how do you practice assertiveness? Practicing assertiveness involves using "I" statements to express your feelings and needs rather than blaming or attacking the other person. It also involves being confident and firm in your communication while still being respectful and open to feedback.

Some good examples of assertive statements you could use are:

"I understand that you have a different perspective, but I stand by my decision."

This statement shows that you're acknowledging the other person's perspective, but ultimately, you are choosing to stick with your own decision. By using "I" language, you are taking responsibility for your choices and feelings. This statement demonstrates a willingness to consider other perspectives while also being confident in your decision-making abilities. It is a respectful way of communicating and can help you assert your own needs and boundaries. Overall, using assertive statements like this can help you avoid self-doubt by allowing you to stand up for yourself and make decisions based on your values and beliefs.

"I feel disrespected when you speak to me in that tone of voice."

This statement communicates to the other person that their tone of voice is causing you to feel disrespected. By using "I" language, you are expressing your feelings and taking responsibility for your emotional response. This can help you avoid self-doubt by giving you a way to express your feelings and set boundaries in a respectful way. Being assertive and direct in your communication means you are less likely to doubt yourself and your feelings. Overall, using assertive statements like this can help you communicate your needs and boundaries in a clear and confident manner, leading to greater self-assurance and self-esteem.

"I understand your concerns, but I have confidence in my abilities to handle this situation."

Here, you acknowledge the other person's concerns, but at the same time, you're ultimately asserting your confidence in your abilities to handle the situation. By expressing confidence in yourself, you can avoid self-doubt and demonstrate your competence. Using assertive statements like this can help you communicate your boundaries and needs in a clear and confident manner, leading to greater self-assurance and self-esteem.

"I value your input, but I have to do what feels right for me.'

In this statement, you are using "I" language to express appreciation for the other person's input while still asserting your autonomy and desire to make your own decisions. Doing so can help you avoid self-doubt and confidently assert your needs and boundaries, even when faced with negative feedback or criticism. Additionally, this statement demonstrates respect for the other person's perspective while still prioritizing your own well-being and decision-making.

"I need you to stop making derogatory comments about my work; it's not helpful or respectful."

This statement uses assertive language to express a boundary and assert your need for respectful treatment. By using "I" language and expressing your own feelings and needs, you are able to communicate your boundaries in a clear and confident manner while still acknowledging the other person's behavior. This can help you avoid self-doubt by setting clear expectations and boundaries for respectful treatment. It can also help improve the overall dynamic between you and the other person. Ultimately, this statement is effective in helping you maintain confidence and self-respect, even in situations where you are faced with negative comments or feedback.

REMEMBER: One of the benefits of practicing assertiveness could be setting boundaries with people who consistently make negative comments or judgments. By asserting your boundaries and expressing your needs, you can avoid feeling overwhelmed or drained by the negative opinions of others.

When you practice assertiveness, you are taking control of the situation and asserting your own value and worth. This can help you maintain a positive self-image and avoid the negative effects of self-doubt. By expressing your needs and opinions in a clear and confident manner, you are also more likely to receive respect and validation from others, which can further boost your self-esteem and confidence.

HOW YOUR OWN PERSPECTIVE CAN LEAD YOU TO MISINTERPRET WHAT OTHERS SAY OR MEAN

People's response to you can be influenced by many factors, including their own beliefs, experiences, and emotions. When you receive feedback or comments from others, it's important to keep in mind that your perspective can sometimes lead you to misinterpret what they are saying. For example, if you are feeling particularly sensitive or insecure about a certain aspect of your work, you may be more likely to interpret even well-intentioned feedback as criticism.

This misinterpretation can then lead to self-doubt as you begin to question your abilities and second-guess your decisions. You may become overly critical of yourself or feel that you are not living up to your expectations or the expectations of others.

To avoid this kind of self-doubt, it's important to approach feedback and comments from others with an open mind and a willingness to consider different perspectives. This means taking the time to really listen to what others are saying rather than jumping to conclusions or assuming that you already know what they mean.

It can also be helpful to ask clarifying questions to ensure that you truly understand the other person's perspective. By seeking to understand rather than defend or justify your position, you can often avoid misinterpretation and the resulting self-doubt.

Overall, recognizing the potential for misinterpretation and being willing to approach feedback and comments with an open mind can help you avoid self-doubt and maintain your confidence and self-assurance.

Key Takeaways

This chapter has helped us understand that certain comments and feedback we get from people are only reactions and don't truly justify who we are or the degree of our ability. In light of this, we've learned the following:

- Strategies to vet/discern every response correctly
- How your perspective can lead you to misinterpret what others say or mean

In the next chapter, we are going to examine your level of self-doubt and the importance of knowing where to start. Let's go!

CHAPTER 6

WHAT IS YOUR LEVEL?

"Doubt kills more dreams than failure ever will."
— Suzy Kassem

Everyone experiences self-doubt to some degree, and it is a normal part of being human.

The level of self-doubt is a measure of how much a person doubts their own abilities, worth, and potential. It can manifest in different ways, such as feeling anxious or uncertain in new situations, avoiding taking risks, and seeking constant validation or approval from others. Excessive self-doubt can lead to low self-esteem, negative self-talk, and a lack of confidence, which can limit personal growth and success.

119

The level of self-doubt can vary from person to person and can be influenced by several factors, including early life experiences, cultural background, social interactions, and personality traits. For instance, individuals who have been exposed to frequent criticism, neglect, or abuse during their formative years may be more prone to self-doubt in adulthood. Similarly, people who grow up in cultures that emphasize humility, obedience, and conformity may develop a stronger sense of self-doubt than those in cultures that promote individualism and self-expression.

Personality traits also play a role in shaping the level of self-doubt. Some people may have a natural disposition to worry, overthink, and ruminate, which can amplify self-doubt. Others may be more optimistic, resilient, and confident, which can mitigate self-doubt. However, it is essential to note that personality traits are not static and can change over time through intentional effort and self-reflection.

The level of self-doubt can also fluctuate depending on the situation and context. For instance, a person may feel confident and competent in their work but doubt their ability to form meaningful relationships. Or, they may feel confident in their physical appearance but doubt their intellectual capabilities. Self-doubt can also be situational, where a person may feel more self-assured in familiar settings but doubt their abilities in unfamiliar ones.

When a person doubts themselves, they often have negative thoughts and beliefs about their abilities and worth. These thoughts and beliefs can create uncertainty, anxiety, and insecurity, leading to a lack of confidence and motivation. However, self-doubt does not necessarily mean that a person lacks self-awareness or a sense of identity. In fact, it is possible for someone who is self-doubting to have a clear understanding of who they are, their values, and their interests.

At the same time, self-doubt can create a distorted view of one's competence. A person who doubts their abilities may underestimate their strengths and overestimate their weaknesses, leading to a skewed perception of their overall competence. For example, a person may excel at a particular skill or task but doubt their ability to perform well consistently, leading them to discount their achievements or shy away from challenging themselves.

Furthermore, self-doubt can create a self-fulfilling prophecy, where the fear of failure or judgment prevents a person from trying new things or taking risks. This avoidance can further reinforce the belief that they are not competent or capable, leading to a cycle of self-doubt and self-limitation.

NOTE: Evaluating one's level of self-doubt is crucial in addressing and overcoming it.

VARIOUS LEVELS OF SELF-DOUBT

Mild Self-doubt

Mild self-doubt refers to a level of self-doubt that is relatively low and does not significantly impact an individual's overall confidence or daily functioning. It is normal for individuals to experience mild self-doubt from time to time, and it can arise in different situations, such as starting a new job, meeting new people, or trying something new.

Let's examine this in a more practical way. Take Jane, for example, who is a recent college graduate that has just started her first job as a marketing assistant. She is excited about her new job, but she also feels nervous and uncertain about her abilities. She worries that she may not be able to keep up with the demands of her new role and fears making mistakes that may reflect poorly on her.

The example of Jane is a clear indication of mild self-doubt. We all express this level of self-doubt when faced with new situations.

Moderate Self-doubt

Moderate self-doubt refers to a level of self-doubt that is more intense and pervasive than mild self-doubt. Individuals experiencing moderate self-doubt may have a general lack of confidence in their abilities or may experience self-doubt in specific areas of their lives, such as work, relationships, or personal goals. Moderate self-doubt can significantly impact an individual's self-esteem, motivation, and overall quality of life.

For example, imagine a person named Tom who experiences moderate self-doubt in his professional life. He has been working in his current job for several years and has received positive feedback from his colleagues and supervisor. However, he still feels insecure about his abilities and worries that he may not be doing a good enough job.

As a result of his self-doubt, Tom avoids taking on new projects or responsibilities, even when they are offered to him. He also tends to overanalyze his work and second-guess his decisions, which can lead to delays and missed deadlines. Tom's self-doubt is impacting his professional growth and may even affect his job security if he does not address it.

Severe/Chronic Self-doubt

Severe/chronic self-doubt is a psychological state characterized by persistent feelings of uncertainty, hesitation, and insecurity about oneself, one's abilities, and one's worth. It is a type of negative self-talk that can undermine one's self-esteem and confidence, leading to a range of emotional and behavioral problems.

People who experience severe self-doubt often have a constant inner dialogue that questions their abilities, decisions, and judgments. They may second-guess themselves frequently, doubt their competence, and feel anxious or fearful about making mistakes or taking risks. This pattern of negative self-talk can be debilitating, causing individuals to hesitate, procrastinate, or avoid challenging situations altogether.

Here are some common characteristics of severe self-doubt:

Self-loathing:

Self-loathing is a common characteristic of severe self-doubt. When someone experiences severe self-doubt and exhibits self-loathing, they may have a deep sense of inadequacy, feeling as if they are fundamentally flawed or defective. They may be hyper-critical of themselves, focusing only on their perceived weaknesses and shortcomings. This constant negative self-talk can erode their self-esteem and lead to feelings of self-loathing.

Individuals with severe self-doubt who exhibit self-loathing may believe they are not good enough, no matter how much they achieve or how much praise they receive. They may attribute their successes to external factors or luck rather than acknowledging their abilities and hard work. This can perpetuate a cycle of doubt, as they feel compelled to constantly live up to an impossible standard.

Imposter syndrome:

Imposter syndrome and self-loathing share a common feature. Imposter syndrome is a psychological phenomenon in which individuals doubt their own accomplishments and fear that they will be exposed as frauds. They may believe their success is due to luck or some outside factor other than their own abilities and hard work.

Individuals with impostor syndrome often experience feelings of inadequacy and self-doubt, despite external evidence of their competence and accomplishments. They may discount positive feedback or attribute their successes to external factors rather than recognizing their own skills and contributions. This can lead to a pattern of self-sabotage, as they may avoid taking on new challenges or opportunities for fear of being exposed as a fraud.

Impostor syndrome can have significant negative impacts on an individual's mental and emotional well-being. It can lead to anxiety, depression, and feelings of isolation. It can also impact their professional and personal relationships, as they may struggle to build trust and connect with others.

Paralysis:

When individuals experience severe self-doubt, they may become overwhelmed with indecision and feel unable to take action. They may question their abilities or their judgment, leading them to become stuck in a cycle of self-doubt and inaction.

This paralysis can have significant negative impacts on an individual's personal and professional life. It can prevent them from taking on new opportunities or pursuing their goals and dreams. It can also impact their relationships, as they may struggle to make decisions or take action in their personal lives.

Paralysis can also lead to anxiety and stress, as individuals may feel stuck and unable to move forward. They may become trapped in negative thought patterns, constantly questioning their decisions and second-guessing themselves.

Isolation:

People who experience severe self-doubt may withdraw from social interactions and isolate themselves from others. This can occur for various reasons, such as feeling unworthy of company or fearing judgment and criticism from others.

Isolation can have a terrible impact on an individual's mental health and well-being. It can lead to feelings of loneliness, depression, and anxiety. It can also affect their personal and professional relationships, as they may struggle to connect with others and build trust and intimacy.

Difficulty accepting compliments:

People experiencing severe self-doubt may struggle to accept compliments because they may not believe they are deserving of them. They may have persistent negative self-talk that convinces them that they are not good enough, so when they receive a compliment, it may feel like a lie.

Individuals with severe self-doubt may believe that they have tricked others into believing that they are competent, smart, or talented and that the compliment is just further proof that they are deceiving others. This belief can be part of the impostor syndrome (discussed earlier), which is common among people with severe self-doubt.

In some cases, individuals with severe self-doubt may also fear compliments because they may feel they are being set up for failure. They may worry that if they accept a compliment, they will be expected to perform at an even higher level, which can be daunting for someone already struggling with such deep insecurities.

HOW TO KNOW WHERE YOU'RE AT

Assessing one's level of self-doubt can be challenging since it is a subjective and multifaceted experience. However, here are a few questionnaires to help you access where you're at in terms of your level of self-doubt:

1. When faced with a challenge or new opportunity, do you typically:

a. ☐Feel confident and excited to take it on?

b. ☐Feel a bit nervous but ultimately confident in your abilities?

c. ☐Feel overwhelmed and doubt your ability to succeed?

2. How often do you compare yourself to others?

a. ☐Rarely or never

b. ☐Occasionally, but not to the point where it affects my self-esteem

c. ☐Frequently and it negatively impacts my self-esteem

3. Do you often find yourself second-guessing your decisions?

a. ☐Rarely or never

b. ☐Occasionally, but I'm able to make decisions with confidence

c. ☐Often, to the point where it affects my ability to make decisions

4. How do you react to criticism or feedback?

a. ☐I am open to feedback and use it to improve

b. ☐I sometimes struggle with accepting feedback, but I try to use it constructively

c. ☐I often feel defensive or take it personally, and it affects my self-esteem

5. When you experience failure or setbacks, how do you typically respond?

a. ☐I view them as opportunities to learn and grow

b. ☐I am disappointed but able to bounce back relatively quickly

c. ☐I become overwhelmed and feel like a failure

6. How often do you experience feelings of self-doubt or inadequacy?

a. ☐Rarely or never

b. ☐Occasionally, but it doesn't significantly impact my daily life

c. ☐Frequently, to the point where it affects my daily life

7. How do you talk to yourself?

a. ☐I am generally kind and compassionate to myself

b. ☐I sometimes struggle with negative self-talk, but I try to counter it with positive affirmations

c. ☐I often engage in negative self-talk and have a difficult time being kind to myself

Scoring:

For questions 1, 2, 3, 4, and 5:

a. = 0 points

b. = 1 point

c. = 2 points

For questions 6 and 7:

a. = 2 points

b. = 1 point

c. = 0 points

Scoring interpretation:

0-5 points: Mild self-doubt

6-10 points: Moderate self-doubt

11-14 points: Severe self-doubt

IMPORTANCE OF KNOWING YOUR LEVEL OF SELF-DOUBT

Knowing your level of self-doubt can be beneficial for several reasons:

Self-awareness: Understanding your level of self-doubt can help you become more self-aware and recognize how it affects your thoughts, emotions, and behavior. This self-awareness can help you identify patterns and triggers that contribute to your self-doubt and develop strategies to manage it more effectively.

Personal growth: Recognizing your level of self-doubt can help you identify areas where you want to grow and improve. For example, if you have moderate or severe self-doubt, you may want to focus on building your self-confidence or practicing self-compassion.

Improved relationships: Self-doubt can affect your relationships with others, leading to insecurity, jealousy, and mistrust. By understanding your level of self-doubt, you can work on improving your relationships by building trust, communication, and healthy boundaries.

Improved performance: Severe self-doubt can lead to avoidance or procrastination, which can negatively impact your performance at work or in other areas of your life. By identifying and managing your self-doubt, you can improve your productivity and achieve your goals more effectively.

REMEMBER: Self-doubt is a common experience that affects people from all walks of life. It can impact our confidence, self-esteem, and ability to achieve our goals. However, by knowing your level of self-doubt, you are on the right track to knowing where to start and how to tackle it.

Key Takeaways

This chapter has been helpful in teaching us the following:

- Various levels of self-doubt
- How to know where you're at
- Importance of knowing your level of self-doubt

Now that you know your level of self-doubt as well as its importance, it's vital to now look at the benefits of conquering self-doubt. In the next chapter, we're going to look at what you stand to gain when you finally overcome self-doubt. Let's keep going!

CHAPTER 7

10 BENEFITS OF CONQUERING

SELF-DOUBT

"…If you can remove your self-doubt and believe in yourself, you can achieve what you never thought possible."
— Roy Bennett

The benefits of conquering self-doubt cannot be overstated. It is true that we all experience self-doubt at some point in our lives. However, what do you stand to gain when you finally conquer self-doubt? Let's find out.

135

BENEFITS OF CONQUERING SELF-DOUBT

1. Increased self-confidence

Increased self-confidence is one of the most significant benefits of conquering self-doubt. When we overcome self-doubt, we start to trust ourselves and our abilities, which leads to an increased sense of self-worth and self-esteem. This, in turn, can result in positive changes in our behavior, relationships, and overall well-being.

Scientific research has shown that conquering self-doubt and increasing self-confidence can have a range of positive effects. For example, a study published in the "Journal of Personality and Social Psychology" found that people who had high levels of self-confidence were more likely to pursue challenging goals and were more successful in achieving them than those with low levels of self-confidence (Bandura, 1986).

Another study published in the "Journal of Applied Psychology" in 2001 by Judge and Bono aimed to investigate the relationship between self-doubt, self-confidence, career success, and job satisfaction. The researchers surveyed 874 employees from various industries and asked them to rate their levels of self-doubt, self-confidence, career success, and job satisfaction.

The study found that individuals who were able to overcome their self-doubt and build self-confidence had higher levels of career success and job satisfaction. Specifically, those with higher levels of self-confidence were more likely to be promoted, had higher salaries, and reported greater job satisfaction.

The researchers also found that self-doubt negatively impacted career success and job satisfaction. Individuals who reported higher levels of self-doubt were less likely to be promoted and had lower salaries than those with lower levels of self-doubt. They also reported lower levels of job satisfaction.

The study provides evidence that conquering self-doubt and building self-confidence is important for career success and job satisfaction. It suggests that individuals who are able to overcome their self-doubt and build their self-confidence are more likely to achieve their career goals and be satisfied with their jobs.

2. Improved decision-making

Improved decision-making is another benefit of conquering self-doubt. When we are plagued by doubt, we tend to second-guess ourselves and make decisions that may not be in our best interest. However, when we overcome this doubt and build self-confidence, we are more likely to make better decisions.

For example, let's consider someone who struggled with self-doubt when making decisions for his family. Perhaps he was hesitant to make decisions regarding their finances or his children's education because he doubted his abilities. As a result, he may have made decisions that were not in the best interest of his family.

However, after conquering his self-doubt and improving his self-confidence, he became more assertive and confident in his decision-making. He was able to make more informed decisions, take calculated risks, and trust his intuition. For example, he may have decided to invest in a new business venture or choose a new school for his children based on careful consideration and research rather than second-guessing himself.

This person's improved decision-making skills had a positive impact on his family. His ability to make sound decisions that were in their best interest helped to build trust and confidence within the family dynamic. He was able to take charge and provide strong leadership, which ultimately led to greater success and happiness for his family.

Research also supports the idea that conquering self-doubt can lead to improved decision-making. A study published in the "Journal of Personality and Social Psychology" in 2010 examined the relationship between self-doubt and decision-making. The researchers conducted three experiments to test their hypothesis that reducing self-doubt would lead to greater confidence in decision-making and risk-taking.

In the first experiment, the researchers randomly assigned participants to either a self-affirmation or a control condition. Participants in the self-affirmation condition were asked to write about their values and what was important to them, while those in the control condition wrote about a neutral topic. After completing the writing task, participants were asked to make a series of decisions, including whether to take a safe or risky bet. The researchers found that participants in the self-affirmation condition were more likely to take the risky bet than those in the control condition, suggesting that reducing self-doubt can lead to greater risk-taking behavior.

In the second experiment, the researchers manipulated participants' levels of self-doubt by asking them to recall a time when they failed a task. Participants were then asked to make a series of decisions, including whether to take a safe or risky bet. The researchers found that participants with lower levels of self-doubt were more likely to take the risky bet than those with higher levels of self-doubt, suggesting that reducing self-doubt can lead to greater risk-taking behavior.

In the third experiment, the researchers examined whether reducing self-doubt would lead to better decision-making. Participants were randomly assigned to either a self-affirmation or a control condition and were asked to make a series of decisions regarding a hypothetical business venture. The researchers found that participants in the self-affirmation condition made better decisions than those in the control condition, suggesting that reducing self-doubt can lead to better decision-making.

Overall, the study provides evidence that reducing self-doubt can lead to greater confidence in decision-making and risk-taking, as well as better decision-making. This suggests that overcoming self-doubt can have significant positive impacts on an individual's personal and professional life.

3. Increased productivity

Conquering self-doubt can lead to increased productivity in many ways. When we are confident in ourselves and our abilities, we are more likely to take action, make decisions, and persevere through challenges. This can help us to achieve our goals more quickly and effectively.

For example, let's consider the story of a person named John. John had always dreamed of starting his own business, but he struggled with self-doubt. He worried that he didn't have the skills, knowledge, or resources to succeed, and he was afraid of failure. As a result, he put off starting his business for years.

However, John eventually realized that his self-doubt was holding him back. He began to take steps to overcome his doubts and build his confidence. He read books on entrepreneurship, took classes to improve his skills, and talked to other successful business owners to gain insights and advice.

As John conquered his self-doubt, he began to take action. He wrote a business plan, secured funding, and launched his company. He faced challenges and setbacks along the way, but he persevered, drawing on his newfound confidence and determination.

As a result of his efforts, John's business began to grow and thrive. He was able to attract customers, hire employees, and expand his offerings. He was also able to develop new products and services, which helped to fuel even more growth.

By conquering his self-doubt, John achieved his goal of starting and running a successful business. He was more productive and effective in his work because he was able to take action, make decisions, and persevere through challenges. His increased confidence and determination allowed him to achieve more than he ever thought possible.

4. Better relationships

Another benefit of conquering self-doubt is having a better relationship. Our confidence can lead us to be assertive, communicate effectively, and set healthy boundaries. This can lead to stronger and more fulfilling relationships with others.

For example, let's consider the story of a woman named Sarah. Sarah had always struggled with self-doubt, especially in her romantic relationships. She was afraid of being vulnerable and expressing her needs and desires, and as a result, she was passive and avoidant in her relationships.

However, Sarah realized that her self-doubt was holding her back from having the kind of relationship she truly wanted. She began taking steps to overcome her doubts and build her confidence. She worked with a therapist to identify and challenge her negative beliefs, and she practiced expressing herself more assertively and honestly with her partner.

As Sarah overcame her self-doubt, she began to experience a more fulfilling and satisfying relationship. She was able to communicate more openly and honestly with her partner, which helped to build trust and intimacy. She was also able to set healthy boundaries and prioritize her own needs and desires, which helped to create a more balanced and equal partnership.

Sarah's increased confidence and assertiveness allowed her to have a better relationship with her partner. She was able to overcome her self-doubt and create a more fulfilling and satisfying connection with someone she loved.

5. Better mental health

Conquering self-doubt can have a positive impact on mental health. Self-doubt can be a significant source of stress and anxiety, and it can lead to negative thought patterns and beliefs about ourselves. When we conquer our self-doubt, we can improve our mental health in several ways.

Firstly, conquering self-doubt can help to reduce stress and anxiety. When we doubt ourselves, we may constantly be worried about making mistakes or failing. This may lead to a cycle of negative thoughts and emotions that can be overwhelming and stressful. However, when we are more confident in ourselves and our abilities, we are less likely to experience these negative emotions and more likely to feel calm and at ease.

Secondly, conquering self-doubt can improve our self-esteem and self-worth. When we doubt ourselves, we may have negative beliefs about our abilities, our worth, and our place in the world. As a result, we may develop low self-esteem and a lack of confidence. However, when we overcome our self-doubt, we can develop a more positive and realistic view of ourselves, which improves our self-esteem and sense of self-worth.

Thirdly, conquering self-doubt can help us to develop better coping skills. Due to self-doubt, we may be more likely to avoid challenges or give up when things get difficult. However, as we become more confident in ourselves, we are more likely to face challenges head-on and persevere through difficult times. This can help us to adapt better coping skills and to build resilience in the face of adversity.

Even research and studies support this assertion. One study that suggests that conquering self-doubt can lead to better mental health was conducted by researchers at the University of Michigan and published in the journal "Social Science & Medicine." The study involved surveying over 800 adults about their levels of self-doubt and their mental health.

The study found that individuals who reported higher levels of self-doubt also reported higher levels of anxiety and depression. However, the study also found that individuals who reported conquering their self-doubt and developing a more positive view of themselves had better mental health outcomes. Specifically, individuals who reported higher levels of self-acceptance, self-love, and self-respect had lower levels of anxiety and depression.

The study also found that individuals who reported overcoming self-doubt and developing a positive self-image were more likely to engage in healthy behaviors, such as exercise, healthy eating, and self-care. This suggests that conquering self-doubt not only leads to better mental health outcomes but also promotes a healthier lifestyle overall.

6. Improved communication

Have you ever been hesitant to express yourself or your thoughts and feelings to others because of doubt, which leads to misunderstandings, conflicts, and unresolved issues?

If so, when you conquer your self-doubt, you can become more confident in yourself and your ability to communicate effectively.

For example, consider a young woman who was afraid to speak up in her relationship because of self-doubt. Let's call her Joan. Joan had been in a relationship with her partner for several months, but she often felt belittled and bullied by him. Despite feeling unhappy and unsupported, she was too afraid to speak up and confront him because of her self-doubt. She feared that if she spoke up, her partner would leave her or think less of her.

However, as Joan began to subdue her self-doubt, she realized that she deserved to be treated with respect and dignity. She began to work on her self-esteem and confidence, and she also started to learn more effective communication skills. She learned how to express her thoughts and feelings in a calm and assertive manner, and she also learned how to actively listen to her partner's perspective.

As a result of her hard work and perseverance, Joan was able to have healthy communication with her partner regarding how she felt about his bullying. She expressed her feelings in a clear and respectful manner, and she also listened to her partner's perspective without getting defensive. Through their open and honest communication, Joan and her partner were able to work through their issues and develop a more respectful and supportive relationship.

7. Great sense of control

Self-doubt can lead to feelings of powerlessness and worry because it makes us feel as though we have no say over our lives or the outcomes. Self-doubt can hold us back from living our best lives and making the best choices, but overcoming it can give us that much-needed empowerment.

A good example of gaining a sense of control by conquering self-doubt is exemplified by David, a man who struggled with self-doubt and anxiety throughout his marriage. He often second-guessed his decisions and worried about whether he was doing the right thing for his family. This led to frequent arguments with his wife, who felt frustrated by his lack of confidence and assertiveness.

However, as David overcame his self-doubt, he gained a greater sense of control over his thoughts and emotions. He learned how to challenge his negative self-talk and replace it with more positive and empowering thoughts. He also worked on developing his communication and conflict resolution skills, which helped him better manage disagreements with his wife.

As a result of his hard work and dedication, David improved his marriage and his overall sense of well-being. He felt more confident in his ability to handle challenges and make decisions that were in the best interest of his family. He also felt more connected to his wife, as they were able to communicate more effectively and work through their issues in a healthier and more productive way.

8. Improved self-esteem

Improved self-esteem is another benefit of conquering self-doubt. When we are able to overcome our self-doubt and achieve our goals, we can feel more confident and proud of ourselves. This, in turn, can lead to a greater sense of self-worth and improved self-esteem.

One study that supports this claim was published in the "Journal of Personality and Social Psychology" in 2011. The study examined the relationship between self-esteem and the experience of overcoming self-doubt. Researchers found that individuals who were able to successfully overcome their self-doubt through challenging experiences reported higher levels of self-esteem than those who did not.

In the study, participants were asked to write about a time when they had overcome self-doubt and achieved a challenging goal. They were then asked to rate their self-esteem before and after the writing exercise. Results showed that participants who had successfully overcome their self-doubt reported higher levels of self-esteem after the exercise than those who had not.

This study highlights the benefit of conquering self-doubt to improve self-esteem. When we are able to overcome our self-doubt and achieve our goals, we can feel more assured in our abilities and more positive about ourselves overall. This can have a good impact on our mental health and well-being, as well as our relationships and professional success.

9. Increased creativity

There is evidence to suggest that we can gain increased creativity when we conquer self-doubt. Self-doubt can limit our willingness to take risks, explore new possibilities, and try out new ideas. When we overcome self-doubt, we become more open to experimentation and are more likely to generate creative ideas.

One piece of scientific research that supports this claim is a study conducted by researchers from the University of California, Santa Barbara, and the University of Chicago, published in the journal "Personality and Social Psychology Bulletin" in 2018. The study examined the relationship between self-doubt and creativity and found that people who experience less self-doubt are more likely to be creative.

The researchers conducted a series of experiments in which participants were asked to complete creativity tasks under different conditions of self-doubt. In one experiment, participants were asked to come up with creative ideas for solving a problem and were then told that their ideas would be evaluated by others. Some participants received positive feedback, while others received negative feedback or no feedback at all.

The results showed that participants who received positive feedback were more likely to generate creative ideas than those who received negative feedback or no feedback. Additionally, participants who were able to overcome their self-doubt and generate creative ideas showed increased activity in the prefrontal cortex, a brain region associated with creative thinking.

This study highlights the importance of conquering self-doubt to increase creativity. When we are not limited by negative self-talk or self-criticism, we are more likely to generate creative ideas and find innovative solutions to problems. By overcoming our self-doubt, we can unlock our creative potential and achieve greater success in various aspects of life.

10. Improved self-awareness

Conquering self-doubt can lead to improved self-awareness because it allows individuals to acknowledge their strengths and weaknesses, recognize their own thought patterns, and gain a deeper understanding of their own values and beliefs. When someone is plagued by self-doubt, they may struggle to see themselves clearly or accurately, and this can prevent them from recognizing their full potential.

For example, a woman who is in an abusive relationship may have been told repeatedly by her abuser that she is worthless or undeserving of respect. Over time, she may internalize these messages and begin to doubt her worth and abilities. However, if she is able to conquer her self-doubt, she may begin to see herself more clearly and recognize that she is not to blame for her abuser's behavior.

As she gains self-awareness, she may realize that she has the strength and resilience to leave the relationship and build a better life for herself. She may also begin to identify patterns in her thinking and behavior that have led her to stay in an unhealthy relationship for so long. By overcoming her self-doubt, she can break free from the cycle of abuse and begin to create a new, healthier narrative for herself.

SELF-DOUBT VS SELF-CONFIDENCE MINDSET

Self-doubt and self-confidence are two opposite mindsets that can significantly impact an individual's life.

Self-doubt is a negative mindset that involves a lack of trust in oneself and one's abilities. Individuals who struggle with self-doubt may feel insecure, anxious, or uncertain about their decisions, actions, or thoughts. They may be overly critical of themselves, have low self-esteem, and struggle with self-validation. Self-doubt can hold people back from achieving their goals, trying new things, or taking risks.

On the other hand, self-confidence is a positive mindset that involves a strong belief in oneself and one's abilities. Individuals who possess self-confidence feel capable, competent, and resilient. They have a positive attitude and believe in their ability to succeed. Self-confidence can help people overcome challenges, take risks, and pursue their goals with determination and resilience.

It's important to note that both self-doubt and self-confidence can be learned and reinforced over time through our experiences and how we interpret them. Negative experiences, criticism, and failures can contribute to self-doubt, while positive experiences, validation, and successes can contribute to self-confidence. Additionally, our thoughts, beliefs, and self-talk can reinforce these mindsets, making them harder to change.

Overcoming self-doubt and developing self-confidence requires conscious effort and self-reflection. It involves challenging negative beliefs and replacing them with more positive, empowering ones.

Below are the major differences between a self-doubt and a self-confidence mindset:

Self-Doubt	Self-Confidence
1. Involves a lack of trust in oneself and one's abilities	Involves a strong belief in oneself and one's abilities
2. Can lead to feelings of insecurity, anxiety, and uncertainty	This can lead to feelings of capability, competence, and resilience
3. Can hold people back from achieving their goals	Can help people overcome challenges and pursue their dreams
4. Involves negative self-talk and a focus on one's weaknesses	Involves positive self-talk and a focus on one's strengths
5. Can contribute to a lack of self-esteem and self-worth	Can contribute to a positive attitude and sense of self-worth

6. Can lead to avoidance of new experiences or risks	Can lead to a willingness to take risks and try new things
7. Can be reinforced by negative experiences, criticism, and failures	Can be reinforced by positive experiences, validation, and successes
8. Can result in self-sabotage or self-destructive behaviors	Can result in productive and proactive behaviors
9. Can lead to a cycle of self-doubt and self-blame	Can lead to a cycle of self-confidence and self-empowerment
10. Requires conscious effort and self-reflection to overcome	Requires conscious effort and self-reflection to develop and maintain

NOTE: These are just some of the many differences between self-doubt and self-confidence. It's important to recognize that these mindsets can be complex and may vary depending on an individual's experiences and beliefs. However, developing a positive mindset and overcoming self-doubt can greatly improve one's quality of life and lead to greater personal growth and success.

Key Takeaways

This chapter has been effective and helpful in learning the following:

- Various benefits of conquering self-doubt
- Self-doubt and self-confidence mindset

In the next chapter, we are going to learn how to replace self-doubt with self-trust. This chapter will provide us with proven steps and strategies to utilize in order to be totally free of self-doubt using the self-trust technique. If you would like to learn these strategies, then let's move to the next chapter!

CHAPTER 8

GET RID OF SELF-DOUBT WITH SELF-TRUST

"A mind that trusts itself is light on its feet."
— Nathaniel Branden

One way to counter self-doubt is through the cultivation of self-trust.

WHAT IS SELF-TRUST?

Self-trust refers to the confidence and belief that one has in their abilities, judgments, and decisions. It is the sense of inner knowing that allows individuals to rely on their own instincts

157

and make choices based on their own values, beliefs, and preferences.

When someone has self-trust, they are more likely to take risks, make decisions more quickly, and feel more comfortable with uncertainty or ambiguity. They are also better equipped to navigate difficult or challenging situations, as they trust their ability to handle whatever comes their way.

WHY SELF-TRUST IS IMPORTANT IN GETTING RID OF SELF-DOUBT

Self-trust provides a foundation of confidence and belief in oneself that can counteract the negative effects of self-doubt. When we trust ourselves, we are more likely to take risks, make decisions, and take action toward our goals, even when we experience self-doubt. Self-trust helps us to recognize our own abilities and strengths and to focus on our potential rather than on our limitations.

On the other hand, when we lack self-trust, self-doubt can become a pervasive and self-reinforcing cycle. We may hesitate to take action, second-guess our decisions, and undermine our own abilities. This can lead to a lack of progress toward our goals and cause frustration and disillusionment.

By cultivating self-trust, we can break this cycle and build a more positive and confident mindset. We can recognize and celebrate our successes, take on new challenges, and learn from our mistakes without being derailed by self-doubt. This can lead to greater fulfillment and satisfaction in our lives.

EFFECTIVE STRATEGIES TO BUILD SELF-TRUST

1. Do What You Say You Are Going to Do

"Do what you say you are going to do" is a simple but powerful strategy to build self-trust. It involves making and keeping commitments to ourselves and others and following through on our promises.

Here is an example of someone who used this strategy to build self-trust and get rid of self-doubt:

Emily was a recent college graduate who was struggling to find a job in her field. She had been applying to jobs for months but had yet to receive any offers. She began to doubt her abilities and wondered if she would ever find a job she enjoyed. She realized that she needed to take action to build her confidence and overcome her self-doubt.

Emily decided to start by setting small goals for herself and following through on them. She committed to spending at least two hours each day searching for jobs, networking with professionals in her field, and practicing her interview skills. She also promised herself that she would apply to at least one job each day, even if it didn't seem like the perfect fit.

By consistently following through on these commitments, Emily built a sense of trust and confidence in herself. She saw that she was capable of taking action toward her goals, even when she didn't feel 100% confident in her abilities. She also began to see small successes, such as receiving interview invitations and positive feedback from networking contacts.

Over time, Emily's self-trust grew stronger, and her self-doubt began to fade away. She continued to set goals for herself, followed through on her commitments, and eventually landed a job in the field she was passionate about. She realized that by doing what she said she was going to do, she had built a foundation of trust and confidence in herself that allowed her to achieve her goals and live a more fulfilling life.

In this way, Emily's example shows how the strategy of "Do what you say you are going to do" can be an effective way to build self-trust and overcome self-doubt. By making and keeping commitments to ourselves, we can build confidence in our abilities, establish trust with others, and get rid of self-doubt.

2. Be Honest with Yourself

Being honest with yourself means acknowledging your true thoughts, feelings, and actions without judgment or denial. This strategy can be powerful in building self-trust because it allows you to be more aware of your strengths, weaknesses, and limitations. By accepting yourself as you are, you can begin to trust yourself and believe in your abilities, which can help you overcome self-doubt.

For example, let's say you tend to procrastinate when it comes to important tasks. By being honest with yourself, you can recognize this behavior and take steps to address it. You may acknowledge that you have a fear of failure, which is causing you to put off completing the task. With this awareness, you can work on building your confidence and developing strategies to manage your fear. As you take action and complete tasks on time, you will build self-trust and confidence in your abilities.

A real-life example of someone who was honest with themselves and built self-trust is J. K. Rowling, the author of the Harry Potter series. Before she wrote the first Harry Potter book,

Rowling had faced a series of setbacks in her personal and professional life. However, she was honest with herself about her passion for writing and her desire to become a published author. Despite numerous rejections from publishers, Rowling continued to believe in her writing abilities and eventually found success with the Harry Potter series. Through her honesty and persistence, she was able to build self-trust and overcome self-doubt to become one of the most successful authors of all time.

3. Do What You Believe is Right

Doing what you believe is right is a powerful strategy for building self-trust and overcoming self-doubt. When you act in accordance with your values and beliefs, you are more likely to feel confident and secure in your decisions. This can help you build self-trust by demonstrating that you are capable of making good choices, even in difficult or uncertain situations.

For example, let's say you are faced with a decision at work that goes against your ethical principles. By doing what you believe is right, you may choose to speak up and address the issue with your boss or colleagues. Although this can be challenging and may even put your job at risk, you can feel confident that you have acted in accordance with your values and beliefs. By doing so, you demonstrate to yourself that you are capable of making difficult decisions and standing up for what you believe in, which can help you build self-trust.

A real-life example of someone who did what they believed was right and built self-trust is Malala Yousafzai. Yousafzai is a Pakistani education activist who was shot by the Taliban for speaking out about the importance of girls' education. Despite the danger, Yousafzai continued to speak out and advocate for the education of girls, eventually becoming the youngest-ever Nobel Peace Prize laureate. Through her actions, Yousafzai demonstrated her unwavering commitment to her values and beliefs, even in the face of extreme danger. By doing what she believed was right, Yousafzai was able to build self-trust and overcome self-doubt, becoming a powerful inspiration to others.

4. Avoid Making Hasty Decisions

When we make decisions too quickly, without fully considering our options or thinking through the consequences, we may later regret our choices or doubt our judgment. By taking the time to carefully consider our decisions and gather more information, we can make more informed choices that align with our values and goals, which can help us build self-trust.

For example, let's say you are considering accepting a job offer from a company that seems promising but is relatively unknown. Rather than rushing to make a decision, you take the time to research the company, speak with current and former employees, and weigh the pros and cons of accepting the offer. By carefully considering all the information, you can make a more informed decision about whether the job is a good fit for you. This can help you build self-trust because you know that you have made a decision based on careful consideration and a thorough analysis of the facts.

A good exemplary figure of this can be linked to Warren Buffett, the billionaire investor, and CEO of Berkshire Hathaway. Buffett is known for his careful and methodical approach to investing, which involves extensive research and analysis before making any decisions. By taking the time to thoroughly research companies and industries, Buffett has been able to make informed investment decisions that have helped him amass a fortune over the course of his career. Through his careful decision-making process, Buffett has demonstrated his ability to make sound judgments, which has helped him build self-trust and confidence in his abilities as an investor.

5. Avoid Criticizing Yourself When Your Decision Doesn't go as Planned

The strategy of avoiding self-criticism when your decision doesn't go as planned is based on the idea that self-doubt often arises from negative self-talk and harsh internal criticism. When we make a decision that doesn't work out, it's easy to fall into the trap of blaming ourselves and focusing on our mistakes. However, this can establish a recurring pattern of self-doubt and negative thinking that is difficult to break.

Instead of criticizing yourself, try to view the situation as a learning experience. Ask yourself what you can learn from the decision that didn't work out and how you can use that knowledge to make better decisions in the future. Focus on what you did well and what you can do better next time rather than dwelling on your mistakes.

It's also important to remember that everyone makes mistakes and experiences setbacks. It's a natural part of the learning process, and it doesn't mean you are a failure or that you lack the ability to make good decisions. By reframing your mindset and focusing on growth and learning, you can eliminate self-doubt and develop greater confidence in your decision-making abilities.

6. Master the Act of Calmness (mindfulness)

Mastering the act of calmness is a powerful self-trust strategy that can help you get rid of self-doubt. Self-doubt often arises when we feel overwhelmed or stressed, which can cloud our judgment and make it difficult to confidently make decisions. By cultivating a sense of calmness, you can reduce stress and anxiety, which can improve your ability to make decisions with clarity and confidence.

One way to cultivate calmness is to take a break when you are feeling overwhelmed or stressed. Sometimes, taking a few minutes to step away from a situation can help you gain perspective and clarity. This can help you make decisions with greater confidence and self-trust.

Scientifically, this strategy has proven to be effective in tackling self-doubt. A study published in 2016 in the journal "Social Cognitive and Affective Neuroscience" supports this claim.

The study found that individuals who could regulate their emotions and remain calm in the face of stress were more likely to have positive self-perceptions and lower levels of self-doubt.

The study involved 41 participants who were asked to complete a task designed to induce stress. Participants were asked to complete a challenging math problem in front of an audience while being timed and receiving negative feedback. Participants' brain activity and emotional responses were measured using functional magnetic resonance imaging (fMRI) and self-report measures.

The results showed that participants who could regulate their emotional responses and maintain a sense of calmness during the stressful task had lower levels of negative self-perceptions and self-doubt compared to those who were less able to regulate their emotions. The researchers found that this was due to increased activity in the prefrontal cortex, a region of the brain that is involved in emotional regulation and executive function.

This study suggests that maintaining a sense of calmness in the face of stress can help individuals reduce self-doubt and negative self-perceptions. By regulating their emotional responses and activating the prefrontal cortex, individuals may be better able to think clearly and make decisions with greater confidence and self-trust, even in challenging situations.

7. Always See Yourself as the Best in Whatever You do

When you see yourself as the best at whatever you do, you approach your tasks and challenges with a confident and positive attitude, which can lead to greater success.

Self-doubt is a common experience that can hold us back from achieving our full potential. When we doubt ourselves, we hesitate to take risks, make decisions, or pursue our goals. This can lead to missed opportunities and a lack of personal fulfillment.

By seeing yourself as the best at whatever you do, you can cultivate a positive self-image and reinforce your confidence in your abilities. This can help you overcome self-doubt and take on new challenges with enthusiasm and determination.

However, it is important to balance this mindset with humility and a willingness to learn and grow. Seeing yourself as the best does not mean that you are perfect or that you have nothing to learn. It simply means that you believe in your abilities and your potential for success.

Michael Jordan is a good example of this strategy. Jordan is widely regarded as one of the greatest basketball players of all time. Throughout his career, he consistently displayed a confident and competitive mindset, often pushing himself to the limit and refusing to let self-doubt hold him back.

Jordan once said, "I've missed more than 9,000 shots in my career. I've lost almost 300 games. Twenty-six times, I've been trusted to take the game-winning shot and missed. I've failed and missed over and over again in my life. And that is why I succeed."

This quote demonstrates Jordan's belief in himself and his ability to overcome failure and self-doubt. By seeing himself as the best, Jordan was able to push himself to achieve great success and become a legendary figure in the world of basketball.

REMEMBER: If Michael Jordan could do it, you can too. By always seeing yourself as the best at whatever you do, you can cultivate a strong sense of self-trust and confidence that will help you overcome self-doubt and achieve your goals.

Key Takeaways

In this chapter, we've been able to cover the following:

- What is self-trust?

- Why self-trust is important in getting rid of self-doubt
- Effective strategies to build self-trust

Now that we've learned how to use self-trust to eliminate self-doubt, let's find out an effective plan to break this cycle and create a healthy self-image and confidence in less than a year!

CHAPTER 9

TIME TO TAKE ACTION

"Action is the foundational key to all success."
— Pablo Picasso

A healthy self-image is essential for overall well-being and success in all aspects of life, including personal relationships, career, and mental health. Therefore, it is essential to take action to break the cycle of self-doubt and build a healthy self-image.

Taking action to break the cycle of self-doubt and build a healthy self-image is important because it allows one to see themselves in a more positive light, which can lead to increased self-esteem, greater resilience, and improved mental health. By overcoming self-doubt, individuals can unlock their full potential and achieve their goals.

Below is a detailed, 1-year actionable plan to break the cycle of self-doubt and create a healthy self-image.

A PRACTICAL 1-YEAR STEP-BY-STEP PLAN FOR BREAKING THE CYCLE OF SELF-DOUBT AND CREATING A HEALTHY SELF-IMAGE AND CONFIDENCE

MONTH 1 – 3: (Day 1 – 90)

GOAL: Acknowledge Your Doubt

Acknowledging your doubt means being aware of and admitting your self-doubt instead of suppressing it. It's important to realize that self-doubt is a natural human emotion and that everyone experiences it at some point in their lives. By acknowledging your doubt, you can begin to understand why it's happening and work to address the underlying issues. This can help you break the cycle of negative self-talk and create a healthier self-image and greater confidence. It also allows you to seek support from others and take proactive steps toward achieving your goals. Remember, self-doubt doesn't have to control you—you have the power to overcome it with self-awareness and self-compassion.

To learn to acknowledge your doubt, follow these steps:

Step 1: Name it (Day 1 – 44)

When we experience doubt, it can often feel overwhelming or confusing. One of the first things we can do to start addressing it is to identify and name it. This means being clear and specific about what we are feeling uncertain about.

For example, let's say you are a student who is feeling anxious about an upcoming exam. Instead of just thinking, "I'm nervous," you might name your doubt more specifically by saying, "I'm feeling unsure about my ability to do well on this exam, and I'm worried that my grades will suffer as a result."

By naming your doubt in this way, you are acknowledging and accepting your feelings, which can help you move forward and begin to address them. It also provides a clearer starting point for exploring your doubts more deeply and identifying potential solutions or strategies to help you feel more confident and prepared for the exam.

Overall, naming your doubt is an important step in developing greater self-awareness and understanding, which can help you take meaningful action to overcome your doubts and build a stronger sense of self-confidence.

Step 2: Explore it (Day 45 – 90)

This means examining your doubts and identifying the underlying causes, beliefs, or assumptions that may be contributing to your feelings of uncertainty or lack of confidence.

Exploring your doubt can help you gain a better understanding of why you are feeling the way you do, which, in turn, can help you develop strategies to overcome it. Here's an example to help illustrate this:

Let's say you have been offered a new job, but you're unsure about whether you're qualified for the position. To explore your doubt, you might ask yourself some questions to help you better understand your feelings. For example:

What specific skills or experiences am I worried about lacking? Are there any past experiences that make me doubt my abilities?

What evidence do I have that suggests I am qualified for this job?

As you explore your doubt, you might also consider gathering additional information or seeking advice from others. For instance, you could talk to a trusted mentor or colleague about your concerns or research online resources to help you develop the skills you feel you may be lacking.

By exploring your doubt in this way, you can gain greater clarity and insight into your feelings and begin to develop strategies to address them. This can help you feel more confident and prepared to take on new challenges and opportunities in the future.

MONTH 4 – 6: (Day 91 – 182)

GOAL: Make a List of Your Positive Qualities

Making a list of your positive qualities can be a powerful tool to break the cycle of self-doubt and create a healthy self-image. It allows you to focus on your strengths and achievements rather than dwelling on your weaknesses and failures.

Also, you can make a list of the positive qualities you wish to have. All of these begin with brainstorming.

NOTE: The same process of brainstorming the positive qualities you possess applies when brainstorming the positive qualities you wish to have.

Step 1: Start by brainstorming (Day 91 – 134)

Brainstorming is a creative process that involves generating a large number of ideas, solutions, or possibilities in a short amount of time. The goal of brainstorming is to come up with as many ideas as possible without worrying about whether they are good or bad, practical or impractical.

In the context of making a list of positive qualities, brainstorming involves allowing your mind to freely explore and identify all the positive qualities that you possess or wish to possess without judging or censoring yourself. You can use different methods of brainstorming, such as writing down your ideas on paper, creating a mind map, or using a brainstorming app or software.

The idea behind brainstorming is that by allowing yourself to freely generate ideas, you can tap into your creativity and come up with more ideas than you would if you were trying to be more focused and analytical. This is important when making a list of positive qualities, as you want to be able to identify as many positive qualities as possible, even if they seem small or insignificant at first.

Once you have generated a large list of positive qualities, you can then go back and review your ideas, eliminate duplicates or similar ideas, and narrow down your list to the most significant and relevant positive qualities that you possess. This can be a helpful exercise in building self-esteem and developing a healthier self-image.

Step 2: Focus on both personal and professional qualities (Day 135 – 182)

Focusing on both personal and professional qualities when making a list of positive qualities is important because our personal and professional lives are interconnected; both contribute to our overall sense of self-worth and self-esteem.

Professional qualities refer to the skills, traits, and achievements that are relevant to your work or career. Examples of professional qualities include being a good leader, having strong communication skills, being knowledgeable in your field, being reliable, and achieving success in your career.

Personal qualities, on the other hand, refer to the characteristics that make you who you are as a person. Examples of personal qualities include being kind, empathetic, patient, honest, creative, and open-minded.

By focusing on both personal and professional qualities, you can create a more comprehensive and balanced list of positive qualities that reflect all aspects of your life. This can help you develop a more holistic sense of self-esteem and self-worth, rather than just basing your self-image on your professional achievements or personal traits.

NOTE: Once you have your list of positive qualities, here are some ways to use it to break the cycle of self-doubt and create a healthy self-image:

Review your list regularly. Make it a habit to review your list of positive qualities every day. This will help reinforce positive self-talk and improve your self-esteem.

Use your list to challenge negative thoughts. When you find yourself thinking negatively about yourself, refer to your list of positive qualities to challenge those thoughts. For example, one of your positive qualities is "compassion." Whenever you feel you didn't do enough to prevent a certain unfortunate event from happening to someone, use this list to remind yourself that you're a kind and compassionate person. Perhaps the situation where you couldn't help the individual was out of your control. Refer to this list to remind yourself of the instances where you've shown kindness and compassion to others in the past. With this, you will get to appreciate yourself and avoid the feeling of self-doubt regarding compassion.

MONTH 7 – 9 (Day 183 – 274)

GOAL: Set Your Own Internal Standards

Setting your own internal standard is a way to break the cycle of self-doubt and create a healthy self-image by defining success and achievements based on your own values and goals rather than external factors or comparisons to others.

Many people fall into the trap of comparing themselves to others, whether it's in terms of their appearance, accomplishments, or social status. This can lead to feelings of inadequacy, self-doubt, and a negative self-image. Setting your own internal standard means defining success and achievement in a way that is meaningful to you and not based on what others think or do.

One example of someone who fell into the trap of comparing themselves to others and overcame it by setting their own internal standard is the American actress, producer, and director, Mindy Kaling. In her early career, Kaling struggled with feelings of inadequacy and self-doubt, especially in comparison to her white male peers in the entertainment industry. However, she later realized that her uniqueness and individuality were her greatest strengths.

Kaling went on to create, write, produce, and star in her own TV show, "The Mindy Project," which showcased her talent and humor while breaking down stereotypes and barriers in Hollywood. By setting her own internal standard and pursuing her vision, Kaling overcame her feelings of inadequacy and built a successful career on her own terms. Her example highlights the importance of self-awareness and authenticity when achieving personal and professional fulfillment.

To set your own internal standard, here are some steps you can take:

Step 1: Create your wanted values and self-worth (Day 182 – 210)

What is important to you? What do you hold dear in life? Your values will be unique to you, so it's important to take the time to reflect on what matters most to you.

Values are the principles or beliefs that guide your decisions and behavior.

To create your values, here's what you need to do:

A. Self-Reflection:

Take some time to reflect on what's important to you in life, what motivates you, and what gives you meaning and purpose. Ask yourself questions like: What do I care about the most? What makes me happy? What do I stand for? What am I passionate about? These questions will act as a guide toward finding your values. Even if you don't have what makes you happy, you definitely should have what you care about most or what you're passionate about. For example, if what you care about most is your family, then you value love and care. The real deal is that you don't need to check all the boxes, just one or two, and you can find your values through it.

181

NOTE: Self-reflection entails taking a quiet moment to yourself and asking yourself questions like:

How do I define my own self-worth and value, separate from external factors?

What qualities and traits do I appreciate and admire in myself?

What accomplishments or experiences have contributed to a positive self-image?

What negative self-perceptions do I hold, and how can I challenge or reframe them?

What actions can I take to cultivate a strong and positive self-image, independent of external validation?

As you answer these questions, pay attention to the emotions and feelings that arise within you. Your values are often closely tied to your emotions, so reflecting on how you feel can help you identify what's truly important to you. Write down your answers and review them to see if any particular themes or values emerge. This can help you identify your underlying values and guide your efforts to make decisions that align with them.

B. Make your priorities:

Making a priority list is a way of identifying the most important tasks, goals, or values in your life. By doing this, you can focus your time and energy on what matters most to you, rather than getting distracted by less important things. This can help you create the self-image that you want because it allows you to align your actions with your values and goals. For example, if you prioritize exercise and health, you will be more likely to make time for workouts and healthy meals to improve your overall body physique, which can contribute to a positive self-image. On the other hand, if you prioritize social media and TV over your health or personal growth, this can lead to negative self-talk and a lack of motivation.

For example, if someone spends hours each day scrolling through social media or watching TV instead of prioritizing their health or personal growth, they may start to develop negative self-talk and a negative self-image. This is because they are not working on the things that truly matter to them align with their values and goals. They may feel guilty or self-critical when they see others on social media with many accomplishments, and this can lead to negative self-talk and a negative self-image because, at that moment, they may begin to measure the person's success with theirs. As a result, constantly comparing themselves to others on social media can contribute to a negative self-image.

Making your priority list is quite easy. All you need to do is understand what you need to achieve. Do you want to create a healthy self-image based on your personal or professional life? In that case, think about what really matters to you. For example, you might desire to gain more confidence in your body's physique. As a result, fitness and a healthy meal plan might become your priorities for the moment. In terms of your professional life, if you want to improve your ability to relate with people fluently in order to boost your self-image and self-confidence when speaking and addressing those at your place of work, then communication skills might become your priority at that moment.

NOTE: The key is to understand what you need to achieve to gain your dream self-image and list those things in order of their importance.

C. Identify your role models:

Think of people you admire or look up to. What qualities do they possess that you find appealing? This can help you understand your own values and the traits you aspire to embody.

For example, let's say you admire your grandfather because he's always been kind and generous to others. You might identify the values of compassion and generosity as important to you based on his example. Alternatively, if you look up to a successful entrepreneur who took risks to build their own business, you might identify the values of ambition, innovation, and perseverance as important to you.

Identifying your role models helps you understand how you want to live your life and the kind of self-image you want to create. For example, if you look up to a particular athlete for their discipline and commitment to training, you might aspire to develop those qualities in yourself.

Overall, thinking about your role models and the qualities or values you admire in them can be a powerful way to identify your own values and create a healthy self-image.

D. Analyze your behavior:

To evaluate your behavior or daily activities, take a look at how you spend your time each day. Are your activities aligned with the self-image you wish to create? If not, think about what changes you can make to ensure your behavior showcases the self-image you want for yourself. For example, if your desired self-image is to develop the ability to make decisions on your own, you might have to check whether you constantly seek validation from others for everything you do. If this is true, you might have to cut down on the habit of frequently asking others about their opinion concerning your actions. This is the first step to achieving your dream self-image of being an independent decision-maker.

To be more specific or sure if your behavior or daily activities represent the kind of self-image you need for yourself, you can ask yourself a few questions like:

How do my daily habits and routines contribute to my overall well-being and personal growth?

Keeping your time usage in check ensures you're spending your time on achieving the self-image you want. For example, as we said above, if you desire to work on your physique by losing weight in order to gain self-confidence as a healthy self-image, yet you constantly scroll through the internet, watching videos of people who wish to add more weight through eating junk food, then your daily habits or activities do not represent the kind of self-image you want for yourself.

How do I respond to setbacks or failures, and am I taking responsibility for my mistakes and learning from them?

If your goal is to achieve a healthy self-image that represents calmness, then making rash decisions when faced with setbacks or failure is a clear opposite of the kind of self-image you want for yourself. The ability to remain calm when making decisions after a setback or failure is a good attribute of someone who wants to achieve a healthy self-image of calmness. When you make decisions when angry or with mixed feelings, it is, most of the time, not the right decision. So, examine how you respond to setbacks or failures and determine if your response represents the self-image you want.

E. Review your list of desired self-images:

After completing all the steps above, the next thing is to refine/review the list you've created that represents your desired self-image. Review it regularly to ensure that your actions and decisions match up to the self-image you desire to create.

For example, let's say you've gone through the previous steps and identified a long list of actions that represent the self-image you desire, including things like honesty, creativity, adventure, compassion, and more. To refine this list, you might ask yourself questions such as:

Does a compassionate self-image (or any other self-image you wish) only need this particular line of action/behavior, or is there anything else I need to align with it to fully represent the self-image?

Am I 100% committed to any of these actions?

How do I build on this particular line of action or behavior in order to fully showcase or align with the self-image I want?

By reflecting on these questions and taking the time to refine your list, you can create a more focused and meaningful set of values that truly represent your desired self-image. This can help guide your decision-making and prioritize your time and energy.

For example, after refining your list, you might end up with values such as love, honesty, and creativity. This smaller, more focused list can help you make decisions and set goals that align with these core values, leading to a more fulfilling and positive self-image.

Step 2: Define success based on your own desired self-image (Day 211 – 242)

Once you have identified the standards that align with your self-image, the next step is to define success based on them. Defining success based on what's important to you means setting your standards for what constitutes a successful outcome or achievement rather than relying on external factors or comparisons to others, which could eventually lead to self-doubt and a negative self-image.

To define success based on the standards you've identified, do the following:

A. Focus on intrinsic motivators:

Focusing on intrinsic motivators is a powerful way to overcome self-doubt and create a healthy self-image. Intrinsic motivators come from within and are driven by personal standards, interests, and goals, rather than external validation or approval from others. By pursuing activities and goals that align with one's personal standards and interests, individuals can build confidence, self-esteem, and a positive sense of self-worth based on their motivations.

Consider the following as good examples of intrinsic motivators:

Pursuing a hobby or activity for the joy of it: For example, taking up painting or writing poetry as a way to express oneself and enjoy the process, rather than solely focusing on external validation or recognition.

Learning a new skill for personal growth: For example, taking a class to learn a new skill or subject, such as cooking or photography, can help build self-confidence and a sense of accomplishment based on personal growth and development.

Helping others for the sake of it: For example, volunteering for a charity or cause that aligns with one's personal values, such as animal welfare or environmental conservation, can provide a sense of purpose and fulfillment based on helping others and making a positive impact.

Setting personal goals based on intrinsic motivators: For example, setting a goal to run a 5K race as a way to challenge oneself and improve personal fitness rather than solely focusing on winning or competing against others.

REMEMBER: By focusing on intrinsic motivators, you can cultivate a sense of personal fulfillment and purpose, which can help overcome self-doubt and create a healthy self-image. By pursuing activities that align with your personal standards and interests, you can build confidence, self-esteem, and a positive sense of self-worth rather than external validation or approval from others.

B. Stay true to the standards that represent your desired self-image:

When defining success, ensure that it aligns with the standards of your desired self-image. If one of your standards for a desired self-image is honesty, for example, then achieving success through dishonest means would not be in alignment with that standard.

Also, staying true to the vision of your desired self-image is an essential step in creating a healthy self-image and subduing self-doubt. Standards are the guiding principles and beliefs that shape an individual's thoughts, behaviors, and decisions. By staying true to your standards, you can build a sense of integrity, authenticity, and self-respect, which can help boost self-confidence and self-esteem.

Make a conscious effort to align your actions and decisions with those standards. This can involve making difficult choices and standing up for your beliefs, even in the face of adversity or external pressure that may push you to act otherwise.

For example, if one of your core standards is honesty, it may be challenging to tell the truth in certain situations where it would be easier to lie or avoid it. However, by staying true to what fully represents your desired self-image (for example, honesty), you can maintain your integrity and build self-respect, even if the outcome is not what you initially hoped for.

By staying true to your standards, you can cultivate inner strength, self-awareness, and self-acceptance, which can help you overcome self-doubt and build a positive self-image. You can also attract like-minded individuals who share your vision and build deeper, more meaningful relationships based on mutual respect and understanding.

Step 3: Avoid comparing yourself to others (Day 243 – 274)

This is very important for building a healthy self-image and overcoming self-doubt. As humans, it is natural to compare ourselves to others, as we often use external markers of success or achievement to measure our own progress or self-worth.

However, constantly comparing oneself to others can lead to feelings of inadequacy or self-doubt, as it is easy to fall into the trap of believing that one's journey or accomplishments are not enough in comparison to others.

Setting one's internal standard can help break the cycle of comparison by focusing on personal values, goals, and intrinsic motivators, rather than external validation or approval from others.

For example, let's say you're a writer and you've just published your first book. It's natural to look at other writers who have achieved greater success, perhaps winning major literary awards or selling millions of copies of their books. If you constantly compare yourself to these writers, you may begin to doubt your abilities as a writer or feel like you will never measure up to their success.

Instead of focusing on external markers of success, you can set your own internal standard by focusing on your progress and achievements. This might involve setting personal writing goals, such as writing for a certain amount of time each day or finishing a certain number of pages each week. You can measure your progress based on these goals rather than on how many copies of your book have been sold or how many awards you've won.

By setting your internal standard, you can avoid the trap of constantly comparing yourself to others and focus on your own journey and progress as a writer. This can help to create a positive self-image, boost your self-confidence and self-esteem, and ultimately lead to greater success and fulfillment as a writer.

To break this cycle of comparison, you need to:

A. Focus on your own journey:

Focusing on your own journey means setting your own goals and measuring your progress based on those goals, rather than constantly comparing yourself to others. When you focus on your own journey, you set your own internal standard for success and progress as opposed to relying on external validation or comparing yourself to others.

Focusing on your own journey can help you cultivate a sense of authenticity, self-awareness, and self-acceptance. By setting goals that are important to you, you can align your actions and priorities with your own values and desires. This can help you build a positive self-image, boost your self-confidence and self-esteem, and ultimately lead to greater fulfillment and satisfaction in your life.

For example, let's say you're interested in fitness and want to improve your physical health. Instead of comparing yourself to others who may have different body types or fitness levels, you can focus on your own journey by setting realistic goals for yourself, such as running a certain distance or lifting a certain amount of weight. You can measure your progress based on your own goals, and celebrate your own accomplishments, no matter how small. By focusing on your own journey and progress, you can build a positive relationship with yourself and create a healthy self-image.

B. Cultivate a growth mindset:

Cultivating a growth mindset means adopting the belief that our abilities and intelligence can be developed through hard work, perseverance, and learning from mistakes. Rather than seeing our abilities as fixed or innate, a growth mindset emphasizes the potential for growth, improvement, and development over time.

When you cultivate a growth mindset, you focus on learning and progress rather than on fixed abilities or talents. You embrace challenges and see failures as opportunities for growth and learning. This can help build resilience, self-confidence, and a positive self-image.

A good example of cultivating a growth mindset is in the workplace. Let's say you've just started a new job, and you're feeling overwhelmed by the new responsibilities and expectations. If you have a growth mindset, you will approach this challenge with the belief that you can learn and grow in your new role over time. You would seek out feedback and guidance from your colleagues and managers and be open to learning from your mistakes and failures.

Rather than comparing yourself to others or worrying about meeting external standards of success, you would focus on your own progress and development. You would set goals for yourself, both short-term and long-term, and measure your success based on your own progress toward those goals. Even when you face setbacks or challenges, you will see these as opportunities for growth and learning and use them as motivation to continue developing your skills and knowledge.

By cultivating a growth mindset in the workplace, you can build a positive and healthy self-image, break the cycle of self-doubt, boost your self-confidence, and develop resilience in the face of challenges and setbacks. You can also demonstrate to your colleagues and managers that you are committed to your own growth and development, which can lead to greater opportunities for advancement and success in your career.

MONTH 10 – 12 (Day 275 – 365)

GOAL: Sustain and Enjoy Your New Self-Image

This is important because you've had an amazing journey so far. By now, you've mastered the act of acknowledging your doubt; you now know your positive qualities and have finally set your own internal standards.

Now you must take some time to appreciate and enjoy the new you—one free of self-doubt and negative self-image.

You now have your positive qualities as well as your own standards and values to hold on to that will can shape your behavior and life.

NOTE: Appreciating and enjoying your new self after overcoming self-doubt and creating a healthy self-image means accepting and loving yourself for who you are. It means recognizing your worth and valuing your unique qualities and strengths. When you have a positive self-image, you are more confident, resilient, and better able to handle life's challenges. You no longer seek validation or approval from others because you are secure in yourself. Instead, you focus on your goals and aspirations, and you are excited about the possibilities of what you can achieve. Ultimately, appreciating and enjoying your new self means living a fulfilling and satisfying life on your own terms.

To appreciate and enjoy your new self, you can do the following:

Step 1: Engage in activities that lighten your mood (Day 275 – 300)

Engaging in activities that lighten your mood can be a great way to enjoy your new self after breaking the cycle of self-doubt and creating a healthy self-image for yourself. It is important to take care of yourself emotionally, and activities that lift your mood can be an essential part of self-care.

One benefit of engaging in mood-lightening activities is that they can help boost your positive emotions, such as joy, happiness, and contentment. These positive emotions can help you feel more confident and optimistic about yourself and your life, which further reinforces your healthy self-image.

Additionally, engaging in activities that lighten your mood can help you reduce negative emotions, such as anxiety, stress, and sadness. This can be especially important after breaking the cycle of self-doubt, as negative emotions may have been a major contributor to your self-doubt. By reducing negative emotions, you can feel more at ease and comfortable with yourself and enjoy your new self even more.

Let's say that after breaking the cycle of self-doubt and creating a healthy self-image, you want to engage in an activity that lightens your mood. You decide to go for a walk in nature, which is one of your favorite ways to relax and clear your mind. As you walk, you feel the sun on your face, the breeze in your hair, and the fresh air in your lungs. You notice the vibrant colors of the leaves on the trees and the sound of birds singing in the distance. You feel a sense of calm and tranquility, and your mind feels clearer and more focused.

As you continue your walk, you start to feel more energized and inspired. You begin to think about some of the goals you have set for yourself, and you feel more motivated to pursue them. You also start to feel more confident about your abilities, and you realize that you are capable of achieving great things. You feel a sense of pride in yourself, and you know that you are on the right path to achieving your dreams.

By engaging in this mood-lightening activity, you were able to boost your positive emotions, reduce your negative emotions, and reconnect with your interests and hobbies. You were also able to reinforce your healthy self-image and enjoy your new self to the fullest.

NOTE: The key is to choose activities that you genuinely enjoy and that make you feel good about yourself. By doing so, you can continue to reinforce your healthy self-image.

In cases where you do not have any basic activity you enjoy, you can practice Step 2 below.

Step 2: Read motivational quotes (Day 301 – 331)

Motivational quotes are an excellent way to boost your confidence and self-esteem after freeing yourself from self-doubt. These quotes are usually short, simple, and inspiring statements designed to motivate and encourage you to take action toward your goals.

When you read motivational quotes, you are exposed to positive affirmations and messages that remind you of your worth, capabilities, and potential. They can help you shift your focus from negative to positive self-talk, which is essential for building and sustaining a healthy self-image.

By regularly reading motivational quotes, you will start to internalize the messages and beliefs that they convey. As a result, you will see yourself in a new light, with a newfound sense of confidence and self-assurance.

Below is how you can use motivational quotes to build on/sustain your new healthy self-image:

A. Create a collection of motivational quotes

Creating a collection of motivational quotes involves gathering a variety of inspiring statements that resonate with you and help you maintain a positive mindset. This collection can serve as a source of inspiration and encouragement when you need a boost of motivation or when you're feeling down.

To create a collection of motivational quotes, you can start by searching online for quotes related to your specific goals or interests. You can also look for quotes in books, movies, or speeches that inspire you. Some people even create their own quotes based on their personal experiences and insights.

For example, let's say you're trying to improve your fitness and lead a healthier lifestyle. You might search for motivational quotes related to fitness and healthy living.

Some examples of motivational quotes you could include in your collection are:

"Believe you can, and you're halfway there." - Theodore Roosevelt

"The difference between try and triumph is just a little umph!" - Marvin Phillips

"Fitness is not about being better than someone else. It's about being better than you used to be." - Khloe Kardashian

Collecting a variety of motivational quotes that inspire and motivate you can create a powerful tool for building and sustaining your healthy self-image. You can then display and repeat these quotes to reinforce positive beliefs and attitudes about yourself and your ability to achieve your goals.

B. Display the quotes

Displaying motivational quotes in a prominent place is a way to keep them visible and accessible, serving as a constant reminder of your new self-image. This can help you stay focused and maintain a positive mindset.

You can display the quotes in various ways, by printing them out and putting them on your fridge, bulletin board, or bathroom mirror. You can also create a digital collection of quotes and set them as your desktop or phone wallpaper.

For example, let's say you're trying to overcome self-doubt and build your confidence. You might choose to display motivational quotes related to self-confidence in a prominent place in your home, such as your bathroom mirror.

Some examples of motivational quotes you could display are:

"Believe in yourself and all that you are. Know that there is something inside you that is greater than any obstacle." - Christian D. Larson

"Self-confidence is the first requisite to great undertakings." - Samuel Johnson

"You yourself, as much as anybody in the entire universe, deserve your love and affection." - Buddha

By displaying these motivational quotes in a prominent place, you are creating a visual reminder of your new self-image aspirations. Every time you see the quotes, you are reinforcing positive beliefs and attitudes about yourself, which can help you build and sustain a healthy self-image.

C. Use the quotes as affirmations

Using motivational quotes as affirmations involves turning them into personal statements that reflect your beliefs and values. This technique can help you internalize the positive messages of the quotes and strengthen your self-image and self-confidence.

To use the quotes as affirmations, you can simply replace the "you" or "they" in the quote with "I" or "me." By doing this, you are creating a personal connection to the quote and making it part of your belief system.

For example, let's say you have a motivational quote that says, "Believe in yourself and all that you are. Know that there is something inside you that is greater than any obstacle." To turn this quote into an affirmation, you can say, "I believe in myself and all that I am. I know that there is something inside of me that is greater than any obstacle."

Another example of a motivational quote that can be turned into an affirmation is, "I am capable of achieving anything I set my mind to." This statement can help reinforce a positive self-image and boost self-confidence.

Using motivational quotes as affirmations supports positive beliefs and attitudes about yourself, which can help you build and sustain a healthy self-image. With time and practice, these positive affirmations can become second nature and help you stay focused on your new self-image, as well as serve as a source of inspiration when you're feeling down.

Step 3: Study biographies of great people you admire (Day 332 – 365)

Studying the biographies of great people you admire can be a powerful way to reinforce your new healthy self-image after breaking the cycle of self-doubt. By learning about the struggles and successes of people you admire, you can gain perspective and inspiration for your own life.

When you study the biographies of great people, you can see that they too faced challenges and obstacles, and that their success was not achieved overnight. This can help you realize that success is often the result of hard work, perseverance, and a positive mindset.

Additionally, reading about the accomplishments of great people can help you see what is possible for yourself. By learning about the challenges they faced and how they overcame them, you can gain insights and strategies for overcoming your own challenges, achieving your goals, and maintaining a healthy self-image.

For example, let's say you have done the work to overcome self-doubt, and you're now working to build a healthy self-image. To assist you in this process, consider reading the biographies of people who have overcome similar challenges and achieved success. For instance, you can read the biography of Maya Angelou, who overcame a difficult childhood and discrimination to become a renowned poet and writer. By learning about her journey, you can gain inspiration and perspective for your own life.

 To use this strategy to maintain your newly created healthy self-image, you can do the following:

Incorporate biographies into your daily routine: Make a habit of reading a few pages of a biography each morning before starting your day. This can help you begin your day with a positive and motivated mindset. Alternatively, you could read a biography before bed as a way to wind down and reflect on the day.

Use biographies as a source of inspiration when facing challenges: When you encounter a difficult situation, or feel discouraged, turn to a biography of a great person for inspiration. Reading about how others have overcome similar challenges can help you stay motivated and keep a positive outlook.

Join a book club or discussion group: Consider joining a book club or discussion group focused on biographies of great people. This can provide a supportive community of like-minded individuals who are also interested in personal growth and self-improvement. Discussing biographies with others can help you gain new insights and perspectives, and can also provide accountability to keep up with your reading and personal development goals.

NOTE: Incorporating biographies of great people into your daily routine, using them as a source of inspiration when facing challenges, and joining a book club or discussion group are just a few ways you can use biographies to maintain a healthy self-image after breaking the cycle of self-doubt. The key is to make reading biographies a consistent part of your growth journey, and to stay open to the insights and inspiration they can provide.

Key Takeaways

In this chapter, we have learned the following:

- A practical 1-year step-by-step plan for breaking the cycle of self-doubt and creating a healthy self-image and confidence

This chapter has been effective and instrumental to our journey of learning how to break the cycle of self-doubt and create a healthy self-image and sense of confidence. Indeed, there is no better way to achieve self-confidence without first breaking the self-doubt barrier.

With the new image you've created for yourself, you can now explore the world and live freely without fear of the restrictions that self-doubt brings!

CONCLUSION

"Love yourself. It is important to stay positive because beauty comes from the inside out."

— Jenn Proske

It is never a coincidence to have made it this far. For this, you deserve massive congratulations for the zeal, passion, determination, and willingness to get to the end of this great book.

This book has been able to teach us what it means to be in self-doubt as well as its triggers, such as past failures and criticisms, unrealistic expectations, perfectionism, comparisons to others, etc. We've learned that being in constant comparison with others can be detrimental to our general well-being and mental health and could, as well, lead to indecisiveness, avoidance, procrastination, and a negative body image, among others.

Interestingly, we learned that to over-compare and compete means focusing only focus on what we lack rather than on our strengths and what we've achieved. This, too, is proven to lead to burnout, stress, anxiety, low self-esteem and self-worth, and ultimately, self-doubt.

Amazingly, this book doesn't stop there. It also teaches us the various levels of self-doubt, such as mild, moderate, and severe/chronic self-doubt, each with its own consequences, such as fear of taking on new experiences, constant questioning of our abilities, as well as self-loathing, imposter syndrome, paralysis, and isolation, among others.

In order to equip us with the passion, willingness, and zeal to continue, this book takes us on a ride to see, feel, and experience the benefits of conquering self-doubt. It tells us that when we're able to conquer our self-doubt, we stand to gain increased self-confidence, improved decision-making, increased productivity, a better relationship, better mental health, improved communication, and a great sense of control, among others.

In addition, we're able to learn how to get rid of self-doubt with self-trust. We learned that when we do what we say we're going to do, as well as being honest with ourselves, we can conquer self-doubt with self-trust.

Lastly, this book has provided an effective and practical step-by-step 1-year plan that encourages us to gradually and steadily break the cycle of self-doubt and create a healthy self-image for ourselves.

Having learned all this, all I can say is:

You are strong and capable, and you have the power to create the life you want.

Your past does not define you. You have the ability to shape your future through your thoughts and actions.

Celebrate your progress, no matter how small. Every step you take towards a positive self-image is an achievement.

Be kind to yourself. Remember that self-care is not selfish, and it's important to take care of your physical, mental, and emotional well-being.

Surround yourself with positive people who uplift and support you. A strong support system can make all the difference in maintaining a healthy self-image.

Keep an open mind and continue to learn and grow. There is always room for improvement, and each day is an opportunity to become the best version of yourself.

REMEMBER: You are capable of achieving great things, and your healthy self-image is the key to unlocking your full potential. Keep moving forward with confidence and belief in yourself.

Now that you have what it takes to conquer self-doubt and build a healthy self-image, go out there and use them!

Thank You!

Thank you so much for purchasing my book! I truly appreciate you taking a chance on this one when you could have picked dozens of other books.

So THANK YOU for your interest and your precious time! I really hope this helped you and has become a benefit to you.

I would like to ask for one small favor. I am very interested to hear your input on my book. **May you kindly consider posting a review on the platform? Posting a review is the best and easiest way for me to keep writing the kind of books that will help you get the results you want.** Also, it will greatly help support the work of independent authors like me. It would mean a lot to me to hear from you.

Again, thank you for taking the time to read my book!

Leave a review on Amazon

REFERENCES

Bandura, A. (1986). Social foundations of thought and action: A social cognitive
theory. Prentice Hall.

Beau, N. (2017). The Negative Thinking Cure: A Simple But Powerful Process That Will Bring You Lasting Happiness, Self-Confidence, and Success. Beau Norton.

Bollich, K. L., Doré, B. P., & Vartanian, O. (2016). Self-doubt and the reward system: Dissociating neural affective responses to feedback based on goal achievement. Social Cognitive and Affective Neuroscience, 11(5), 774-782. doi: 10.1093/scan/nsw015

Buunk, B. P., & Gibbons, F. X. (2007). Social comparison: The end of a theory and
the emergence of a field. Organizational Behavior and Human Decision Processes, 102(1), 3-21. https://doi.org/10.1016/j.obhdp.2006.09.007

Cameron, G. (2018). Stop Doubting Yourself and Find Your Inner Greatness: Instill Powerful Inner Beliefs, Build Confidence and Self-Esteem and Destroy Self-Doubt. R&C Publishing.

D'Ambrosio, M. P., Bakula, D. M., & Brown, J. D. (2019). "I doubt, therefore I am":
The impact of self-doubt on mental health. Social Science & Medicine, 222, 305-311. https://doi.org/10.1016/j.socscimed.2018.12.023.

Denise, J. (2017). Banish Your Inner Critic: Silence the Voice of Self-Doubt to Unleash Your Creativity and Do Your Best Work (A Gift for Artists to Combat Self-doubt and Listen to Their Inner Voice). Mango.

Denny, B. T., Inhoff, M. C., Zerubavel, N., Davachi, L., & Ochsner, K. N. (2016). Getting over it: Long-lasting effects of emotion regulation on amygdala response. Social Cognitive and Affective Neuroscience, 11(2), 227-236. https://doi.org/10.1093/scan/nsv102

Judge, T. A., & Bono, J. E. (2001). Relationship of core self-evaluations traits--self-esteem, generalized self-efficacy, locus of control, and emotional stability--with job satisfaction and job performance: A meta-analysis. Journal of Applied Psychology, 86(1), 80–92. doi: 10.1037//0021-9010.86.1.80

Kaufman, S. B., Quilty, L. C., Grazioplene, R. G., Hirsh, J. B., Gray, J. R., Peterson, J. B., & DeYoung, C. G. (2018). Openness to experience and intellect differentially predict creative achievement in the arts and sciences. Personality and Social Psychology Bulletin, 44(11), 1495-1511. https://doi.org/10.1177/0146167218771203

Kristin, N. (2011). Self-Compassion: The Proven Power of Being Kind to Yourself.
HarperCollins.

Koole, S. L., Smeets, K., van Knippenberg, A., & Dijksterhuis, A. (2010). The cessation of rumination through self-affirmation. Journal of Personality and Social Psychology, 98(5), 834-846. doi: 10.1037/a0017620

Lockwood, P., & Kunda, Z. (1997). Superstars and me: Predicting the impact of role models on the self. Journal of Personality and Social Psychology, 73(1), 91-103. doi: 10.1037/0022-3514.73.1.91

Louisa, J. (2017). Wire Your Brain for Confidence: The Science of Conquering
Self-Doubt. Louisa Jewell.

Mamuzo, A. (2021). How to Overcome Low Self Esteem and Self-Condemnation.
Jessie Addison.

Marc, R. (2022). Love Yourself First! Boost Your Self-esteem in 30 Days. How to Overcome Low Self-esteem, Anxiety, Stress, Insecurity, and Self-doubt. Maklau Publishing.

Marshall, J. M., Dunstan, D. A., & Bartik, W. (2015). Examining the relationship between self-talk and symptoms of depression and anxiety. International Journal of Cognitive Therapy, 8(4), 323-336. doi: 10.1521/ijct_2015_08_06

Paul, K. (2019). Imposter Syndrome: Eliminate Self-Doubt, Develop Confidence, and Leave Anxiety in the Past. Paul Kembly.

Park, L. E., Crocker, J., & Mickelson, K. D. (2011). Punishing doubts: How self-doubt enhances social conformity. Journal of Personality and Social Psychology, 100(4), 582-604. https://doi.org/10.1037/a0021953

Sakulku, J., & Alexander, J. (2011). The Impostor
Phenomenon. Journal of Vocational Behavior, 79(3), 565-577.
doi: 10.1016/j.jvb.2011.02.018

Schmeichel, B. J., Vohs, K. D., & Baumeister, R. F. (2010).
Intellectual performance
and ego depletion: Role of the self in logical reasoning and other
information processing. Journal of Personality and Social
Psychology, 99(2), 285-301. https://doi.org/10.1037/a0018698

Som, B. (2018). Living Beyond Self Doubt. Som Bathla.

Yeager, D. S., Johnson, R., Spitzer, B. J., Trzesniewski, K. H.,
Powers, J., & Dweck, C. S. (2014). The far-reaching effects of
believing people can change: Implicit theories of personality
shape stress, health, and achievement during adolescence.
Journal of Personality and Social Psychology, 106(2), 267–283.
https://doi.org/10.1037/a0036335

Printed in Great Britain
by Amazon

24614446R00131